Bruce Van Natta had a major miracle from God. Now God has chosen him to mentor you in the supernatural. He and his book are the "real deal."

—SID ROTH
HOST, *IT'S SUPERNATURAL*

Bruce Van Natta's life has been shaped by God's miracles. These amazing stories of healing, rescue, and hope will inspire you to live a supernatural life of victory every day.
—DR. JAMES L. GARLOW
PASTOR, RADIO HOST, AND COAUTHOR OF *NEW YORK TIMES* BEST SELLER *CRACKING DA VINCI'S CODE*

You can't be in the presence of Bruce Van Natta and not be profoundly affected by his authentic spirit. He's a man with an unusually heavy anointing on his life because he's experienced the miracle power of God in a way that few of us have. His new book, *A Miraculous Life*, reflects that same anointing along with offering rare insights into the spiritual realm that can surely help us defeat the giants that threaten to destroy our lives! A must-read for anyone who desires more of the power and presence of God in their life.

—MAX DAVIS
AUTHOR OF *THE INSANITY OF UNBELIEF: A JOURNALIST'S JOURNEY FROM BELIEF TO SKEPTICISM TO DEEP FAITH*

As Bruce's pastor I can attest to his integrity, knowing that he reports with accuracy the miracle testimonies contained in this book. He is a man of character and principle who is relational and personable with people. He possesses a Christlike compassion and demonstrates a genuine love and concern for others, especially for those sick, afflicted, and oppressed by the devil. He has answered the call of God and is serving the purpose of God for this generation.

—MATTHEW J. MALLEK
FOUNDER AND SENIOR PASTOR OF GOOD NEWS FELLOWSHIP CHURCH, STEVENS POINT, WI
FOUNDER AND PRESIDENT OF GOOD NEWS FELLOWSHIP NETWORK OF CHURCHES AND MINISTERS

I am so excited for this book to be in the hands of God's people. Bruce's personal testimony teamed with God's Word and miracles from all over the world remind us that God is still on the move in a big way. The church needs to be refreshed in the knowledge that our Lord still moves mountains today, Jesus is still madly in love with His bride, and He is able to do exceedingly abundantly more than we could ever imagine. This book is a gift straight from the throne room of our loving Savior.

—AUDRA HANEY
PRODUCER, *THE 700 CLUB*

A Miraculous Life by Bruce Van Natta is a book you can't put down once you start to read it. Bruce tells of a lifestyle of the miraculous that he has experienced, and he wants to help you experience it as well. The greatest miracle of all is what he has done in response to God's divine intervention in his life. This is a ministry that truly awakens our hearts to the reality that Jesus Christ is the same yesterday, today, and forever (Heb. 13:8). You will hear the heartbeat of the Holy Spirit on every page.

—JIM MACHEN
SENIOR PASTOR AT CHURCH OF THE OPEN DOOR, CLINTON, IA
BOARD MEMBER OF THE INTERNATIONAL CHURCH OF THE FOURSQUARE GOSPEL

Bruce Van Natta

A Miraculous Life

True Stories of Supernatural
Encounters *With* God

Bruce Van Natta

A Miraculous Life

True Stories of Supernatural
Encounters *With* God

CHARISMA
HOUSE

Most CHARISMA HOUSE BOOK GROUP products are available at special quantity discounts for bulk purchase for sales promotions, premiums, fund-raising, and educational needs. For details, write Charisma House Book Group, 600 Rinehart Road, Lake Mary, Florida 32746, or telephone (407) 333-0600.

A MIRACULOUS LIFE by Bruce Van Natta
Published by Charisma House
Charisma Media/Charisma House Book Group
600 Rinehart Road
Lake Mary, Florida 32746
www.charismahouse.com

Unless otherwise noted, all Scripture quotations are from the Holy Bible, New International Version. Copyright © 1973, 1978, 1984, International Bible Society. Used by permission.

Scripture quotations marked KJV are from the King James Version of the Bible.

Scripture quotations marked NKJV are from the New King James Version of the Bible. Copyright © 1979, 1980, 1982 by Thomas Nelson, Inc., publishers. Used by permission.

Cover design by Gearbox Studio

Visit the author's website at www.sweetbreadministries.com.

Library of Congress Cataloging-in-Publication Data
Van Natta, Bruce.
  A miraculous life / Bruce Van Natta. -- 1st ed.
       p. cm.
  ISBN 978-1-61638-679-5 (trade paper) -- ISBN 978-1-61638-680-1
(e-book)
  1. Van Natta, Bruce. 2. Christian biography. 3. Miracles. 4. Astral
projection. I. Title.
  BR1725.V235A3 2013
  248.4--dc23

                        2012035679

18 19 20 21 22 — 9 8 7 6 5 4
Printed in the United States of America

This book is dedicated to the living triune God. May His name be glorified in these pages, and may the people who read this book come to know Him better as they experience the miraculous life He has made available for all.

CONTENTS

Preface

Great faith comes from great fights—
Great testimonies come from great tests—
Great triumphs come out of great trials—
                                —Smith Wigglesworth

I N November of 2006 I had a horrible accident where at the point of death I had an out-of-body experience. During that out-of-body experience the Lord allowed me to see the two angels He sent to save my life. I spent much of the next year in the hospital having five major operations and enduring many days when I could not even get out of bed because of the severe pain and injuries. I shut down my successful business as a diesel technician and finally submitted to God's call on my life for full-time ministry. Somehow I ended up ministering a handful of times in between hospital stays and operations that year.

On January 1, 2008, we officially started Sweet Bread Ministries after only being out of the hospital a few weeks since my last major operation. We watched in awe as the Lord used this testimony to bring many to salvation as well as to bring healing to many others. It became clear that God was turning this tragedy into a triumph!

During that May, while still recovering at home, the Lord gave me a dream that directly related to the book you are holding in your hands right now. It, as well as some other supernatural things that happened, proved to me how important He thinks this message is.

In the dream I was at a gate in an airport waiting to board a large jet airliner for a very important flight. I was looking for my suitcase but couldn't seem to find it, and for some reason I could tell that many people would be hindered and their plans would not, and could not, continue until that plane took off. A faceless person from behind the desk pointed to a large round clock and said that I needed to gather my things because the plane was going to take off in exactly three minutes. I felt a sense of urgency as well as a sense of not being prepared as I realized others were counting on me and waiting on me.

Immediately the dream ended, and I woke up with a very strong presence of the Lord in my bedroom. I asked Him what the dream meant, and the Holy Spirit very clearly told me to "do the math." I was puzzled as there was only one number given in the dream: the three minutes until the plane was to take off. The Holy Spirit then reminded me that a day for the Lord was like a thousand years for me and again told me to "do the math."

I got up from the bed, sat down at my desk, and began to plug these numbers into the only algebra formula I could remember from my schooling. If a day to the Lord was like a thousand years to me, then the question was: What is three minutes to the Lord in my time? After using the equation, I came up with the answer of two years and twenty-some days. I asked the Lord if I had come up with the right answer, and the Holy Spirit said that I had and that I was to now write it down in my journal. So I chronicled the dream and its interpretation in my journal, ending with the statement that something very important was going to happen for the ministry and for other people near the end of June 2010. The final sentence written in the entry simply says, "Empowered ministry is close!"

I had completely forgotten about this dream by the time two years had passed, but the Lord used another situation to cause me to go back and read through the journal and that particular entry. I realized that there were only about two weeks left until the appointed time, so I marked it off on my calendar.

When that week arrived, I waited in great expectation. My answer to the dream came in the form of a phone call from the Charisma House Book Group. Someone very high in the publishing arm of their company had recently read a story about me in *Charisma* magazine and felt led by the Lord to extend an offer to me to publish my next book.

The person who called said they had some ideas as to what they were looking for, and those ideas "just happened" to fit right in with what the Lord had clearly told me my next book was to be about in the months preceding this call. The ideas they presented to me included my telling testimonies of God's power in our everyday life. It was clear that this uninvited, unexpected offer was clearly the sovereign hand of God at work and the beginning of the fulfillment to the dream!

I was told that we would now have to go through the process where the different departments would need to put their stamp of approval on the project before it could proceed. The preliminary meeting on the project was in July, and the final decision would be made at a meeting on October 22.

I had a doctor appointment on that day for a routine checkup. It had been nearly four years since the accident, and the doctor was amazed that, according to the blood work and various test results, I was back to almost perfect health.

As I drove home from the hospital, I was in a glorious mood. The checkup was more proof of my miraculous healing. I knew that the meeting at the publisher was probably over by now, and there should be a message on my answering machine with more "good news" from them.

My entire family was gone that day when I left the house and would not be home until much later in the day. This meant that the only one home would be Daisy, our one-hundred-pound yellow Lab who is the seventh member of our family. During my extended time of bed rest after the accident, she did not leave my side and became like my shadow. Because of this she got very used to having me around, so when I do leave, she doesn't like it at all. This also means that when I get home, she always meets me at the door with loads of attention and barking.

When I got home and unlocked the door going into the main room of our house that day, I was completely dumbfounded by what happened. First of all Daisy wasn't barking at me from the other side of the door, which was very odd. When I opened the door, I immediately could see her sitting in front of one of the two large sliding glass doors that are on the opposite end of that room. She was facing the glass with her back toward the room and me. I called her name, but she didn't budge, which would never happen normally.

As I started to walk closer, I stopped, shocked by what I saw. There was a bird sitting right next to her on the floor, also looking out the window! I could now see several vertical smears on the sliding glass door from one end to the other. At that moment the bird flew up about two feet off the floor and began to flutter against the glass. As it did, Daisy put her nose underneath the fluttering bird and began to gently nudge it upward as if trying to help it fly away. After a bit the bird sat back down on the floor, evidently tired, and the two of them just continued to motionlessly look out the window side by side.

It was now apparent that the smears on the glass were from Daisy's nose as she was nudging the bird upward, trying to help it fly. If this alone doesn't shock you, it is because you don't know Daisy. She is a great dog that loves living out here in the woods, but I have to admit she has kind of a dark side to her. As loving and nice as she is to people, she can't control herself from trying to kill small animals. Because of her breed, she is continually hunting rabbits, squirrels, chipmunks, birds, and even mice. It doesn't matter what or where the animal is; she believes it is her job to find and exterminate it. It is the one bad habit we have never been able to break her of. It is part of her nature, and here she was, not trying to kill this bird at all but instead looking as if she were trying to help it get out! It made no sense at all.

My mind raced as I began to contemplate how this bird even got into our house in the first place. There were no open doors or windows, and even if there were, each one has a screen. We didn't have any chimneys or openings of any kind that a bird could get in through. No one else could have been inside our house as it was completely locked up until I got back. In all the years since we had built the house, we had never had a single bird get in, and I sure didn't see this bird in the house when I left. The bird didn't appear to be hurt at all, and interestingly I couldn't readily identify what kind of bird it was either. It looked much like a common mourning dove, but it did not have the right colors as it was mostly white with some dark areas on top of the wings. I had never seen a bird like it before, which was odd after growing up in the country as an avid outdoorsman and living in the woods almost my whole life.

As I looked with utter disbelief at my dog and this bird peacefully sitting next to each other on floor of my enclosed home, a very strong presence of the Lord rolled in. Then the Holy Spirit spoke to me. He said simply that I needed to release the bird. I walked up to the door fully expecting the bird, which was now at my feet, to try and fly away from me, but it didn't move. I knelt down and looked closely at the bird. It appeared to be an adult but strangely didn't seem afraid of me at all. In fact, I stroked the back of its head without it moving. Even as I did this, it didn't take its gaze from looking out the window. I couldn't help but wonder what could be wrong with this bird, or my dog for that matter, and once again the Holy Spirit said that I needed to release it. I stood up and unlocked the sliding glass door and then slid it open, but to my amazement neither the bird nor my dog moved a muscle.

Again the Holy Spirit told me to release the bird, so I said aloud, "You are free to go. You are released." At that point the bird flew effortlessly and gracefully away into the woods and out of sight. The whole event had a very surreal feeling to it, and I found myself repeating over and over, "I can't believe that just happened." The smeared glass window and small spots of bird poop on the floor proved it had. I pulled out our *National Audubon Society Field Guide to North American Birds* and searched for this strange bird, but I couldn't find anything in the pictures that matched up. As I tried to picture the simple white bird again, the dark wing markings seemed to blend in my mind, and I just couldn't distinguish them from any of the ones in the book.

There was still a strong sense of the Lord's presence, and I asked Him what this was all about. I felt led to sit down at my desk and turn on the computer and check phone messages and e-mails. There was a phone message from Charisma House saying that the meeting went well, they were very excited about the book, and the project was a go-ahead. I also found an e-mail from someone at *Charisma* magazine who had sent a link to their homepage, and there on the homepage was a mostly white bird that looked just like the one that had minutes before been in my house! I looked over on my shelf and realized it was also on the cover of one of their most recent magazine issues—a mostly white dove-looking bird with undistinguishable color markings on the wings!

The Holy Spirit spoke again and told me what had just happened was supernatural and that it was prophetic of the message that was to be in this book project. This was a message that was so powerful it could bring supernatural peace where there had been struggles, victory where there had been loss, and life where there had been death. (My dog not trying to kill the bird as she normally would have done, but trying to help it, now made perfect sense.) The bird was white and black because this message is the plain truth, but the wing markings were indistinguishable, portraying the great confusion that surrounds this subject. Graceful freedom would come for the captive when this message was released, and it was also clear that God was saying now was the time to release this message and He was telling me to do it.

The Lord also reminded me of the original dream He had given me about this book—how there were scores of people who were waiting, how they were being hindered, and the plans He had for them were not being fulfilled until this message was released from the gate.

This book contains that message wrapped up in the various testimonies you will read. It is a message so potent that it will change your life forever if you embrace it. God wants to empower you to live a life of victory over the enemy no matter what happens, walking in the miraculous and experiencing the supernatural as a part of "normal" living not only for your own benefit but also so you can show a lost and hurting world who God really is!

—Bruce Van Natta

Introduction

IRST CORINTHIANS 4:20 states that the kingdom of God is not a matter of talk but of power. This is just one of many verses found in the Bible that gives us insight into what is available to all believers. God wants us to stay plugged into Him so that we can live a supernatural life of victory. Jesus said that our enemy the devil comes to steal, kill, and destroy, but He came that we might have life and have it to the full (John 10:10). He wants us to live the abundant life. We should expect the full, miraculous, and abundant life to be normal Christianity. This book is filled with stories of what the miraculous looks like in daily life, and it gives key points to help believers become empowered to walk in supernatural triumph themselves, regardless of the circumstances or even short-term outcomes.

Revelation 12:11 says, "They overcame him by the blood of the Lamb and by the word of their testimony." We know from the context that the "him" is Satan, or the devil. The verse clearly says that we overcome him first and foremost by the blood of the Lamb, which is the finished work of the cross carried out by Jesus Himself. It is the only reason we can expect to have victory in any area of our lives.

The next phrase says that they also overcame the devil by the "word of their testimony." The testimony of what Jesus did while He was here on this earth and the testimony of what He continues to do in people's lives today are so powerful that they are able to completely overcome our main adversary, the devil. That is one of the two reasons why this book is full of testimonies! They are powerful!

Think of your favorite Bible stories; what are they? They are testimonies of what God did or accomplished in somebody's life. When read, these testimonies have the ability to build faith in a person; that is what makes them so powerful.

We also learn something very interesting about testimony in Revelation 19:10. It says in the last sentence of that verse that "the testimony of Jesus is the spirit of prophecy." This is how I see that play out in daily life. Let's say someone has a deaf ear they want the Lord to heal. I will begin to tell them about several specific people I have personally seen the Lord heal from deafness, sometimes quoting first names, cities, or churches where it has happened, or I will bring up a Bible account where it happened.

I will then very often tell them God loves all people equally, even as much as He loved Jesus, according to John 17:23. I go on to tell them that if He healed all the people I just told them about from deafness, then we should be able to expect that He would do it for them also. In other words, the testimony of what Jesus did for the people I just told them about and the testimonies we read about in the Bible are prophetic of what He wants to do for them! This is the second reason this book is full of testimonies: they are prophetic! While we may not know God's timetable or tactics for healing someone or getting them through a problem, we can know from the Bible that it is His will to be our healer and Redeemer one way or another, sooner or later. Jesus declared He came to set the captive free! (See Luke 4:16–19; John 8:36.)

I find that the Lord has me use this tactic quite often when ministering to people as it has the ability to raise their faith to a level where they can believe there is a good chance God will do for them what He has done for others. If they have a broken relationship, I tell them about people who have had relationships restored. If they are having some type of spiritual problem, I will tell them about people who have been given victory through Jesus. If they have some type of physical problem, I will tell them about people who have been healed from the same thing. If they are dealing with an emotional issue, I will tell them about people who have been set free from the same difficulty. There haven't been too many things we haven't seen the Lord take care of at least once, and if I can share even one testimony with the person about somebody whom God has helped through the same problem he is encountering, I will do it.

As you read the testimonies in this book, take them to heart and apply them to your life. I pray that as you do, two things will be accomplished in you.

First, I pray you will realize God wants to empower you to live a life of victory and that He has supplied everything you need in order for that to happen, no matter what the problem is or how bad it looks. God says you are more than a conqueror (Rom. 8:31–39)!

Second, I pray your faith in God will be raised to the point of boldness and that you will understand God wants to use each of us to accomplish His will here on this earth, including "little ol' you" (Acts 4:29–31).

I have heard a woman I know who runs an orphan ministry quote an early church father several times. She says, "Always preach the gospel, but only use words when necessary." She understands the best evangelistic tool available is living a victorious life, one that overflows with the love and power of God regardless of what the circumstances are.

If we make ourselves available to God and stay in step with His will, He will not only guide and bless our lives, but also He will use us to be His hands and feet here on this earth. We will not only live a life of victory, but also we will get to see other people saved, healed, and delivered as well! Hallelujah!

Let me give you an example.

Early in the ministry I was invited to share my testimony at a summer camp for high school youth. It was a weeklong camp, and I spoke on the morning of the final day of camp. For the last week these young people had been swimming, canoeing, hiking, as well as staying up late around the campfire. So needless to say, they were very tired by the morning of the last day.

There were eighty high-school-age youth, ten college-age counselors, and three pastors in attendance that morning. As I began to give my testimony, several heads went down on the tables and a handful of people instantly went to sleep. Let me stop right here and say that this almost never happens to me. I minister on average to over ten thousand people per year in person, and while I might see the occasional sleeper in a place, it is rare because of the incredible testimony the Lord has done in my life. Things like being crushed in half by a falling truck, giant angels, and life-after-death stories tend to keep people's attention.

Within the first ten minutes of talking, there were at least ten sleepers. I began to complain to God in my head as I continued to speak. After a few more minutes the Holy Spirit told me to just quit talking, so I did. Within just a minute or two some of the sleepers began to wake up because the background noise was gone. The sheer silence got their attention.

I asked the Lord what He wanted me to do at this point. He said, "Pull up your shirt and begin walking around showing them your scars, but don't say a word." As I did this, many of the people who saw my scars up close began to gasp and make groaning noises that were loud enough to wake up a few more of the sleepers.

Standing there in the awkward silence, I asked the Lord what He wanted me to do next, and the Holy Spirit told me to ask them the question, "Who wants to see Jesus do a miracle right now?" I hate to admit it, but I was not as readily obedient to this command as I had been to the first two. You see, this camp was run by a Christian denomination that often teaches God no longer does miracles today in the same way He used to. I knew that even them having me share my testimony was something out of the ordinary for them and probably was quite a stretch for most of the people there.

Again the Lord told me to ask them the question "Who wants to see Jesus do a miracle right now?" So I said it rather quietly over the microphone, at which point the Holy Spirit told me to say it again, only to do it much louder this time. To the shock of everyone there, including myself, I did say it again at the volume of almost a yell: "Who wants to see Jesus do a miracle right now?" I watched as several of them looked at each other in bewilderment and surprise because of what I had just said and done.

As you can imagine, there was no longer anyone left sleeping. Standing there in the absolute hush I watched as very slowly each person raised their hand, except for the three pastors in the back row. Every eye in the place was on me, and you could have heard a pin drop in the deafening silence.

Completely dependent upon the Holy Spirit at this point, I asked Him to please do something quick. Immediately He began to give me words of knowledge about certain physical problems people in attendance had. As I spoke each specific health concern out, I told the person to whom it applied to come forward immediately. There were now several people standing across the front of the room.

The first person in line was a girl I will call "Suzy Cheerleader." You probably know the type of person I am talking about. This was early morning on day seven of summer camp, and yet her hair, nails, and wardrobe were perfect. She was a very pretty girl, and you just knew she was popular and everybody wanted to be her friend.

She had pain in her toes, and when I kneeled down and looked at her feet, I was able to see her toes were slightly curled under from some type of medical condition. I prayed over her feet, and immediately the toes came out straight and her pain left. When this happened, she began to sob and call out to God loudly, which shocked the rest of the group, as apparently this sort of thing never happened in their churches. To them it was unthinkable that "Suzy" would make a scene or lose her cool composure.

Almost everyone in the place got to their feet, and several people began to crowd around the front, standing around those who had been called forward for prayer.

The next person who had been called out was a girl who had almost constant pain in her knee. She had surgery on it at some point, and the doctors had installed some screws to hold things together. In addition to the "normal" pain she dealt with in her knee, whenever she would bend down on it or bump it just right, the knee would hurt badly and perfect red circles would show up where the heads of the screws were just underneath the skin.

I placed my hands on her knee and prayed over her in the name of Jesus. She got excited and said all the pain had left immediately. I asked her to get down on her knee and see what it felt like now. She very gingerly got down and began to rock it back and forth, trying to hit the tender spots where the screws were, but she couldn't get it to hurt this time.

To my shock she began to lift her knee off the floor and then slam it down with a lot of force. After she did this a couple of times, I stopped her and asked to look at the knee. This time there were no red circles at all; they were completely gone, and so was all her pain. This girl too started crying and thanking God out loud just as the last one had. The whole group was now crowded to the front of the room, and the atmosphere felt almost explosive as some people began to clap and laugh with joy as others started to weep in the strong presence of God that was there.

To say I got excited at that point would be a huge understatement. In fact, I pretty much lost it as I began to jump up and down and yell out, running back and forth. It was clear to me every person who had been called out was going to get gloriously healed and God was making a huge statement. Unfortunately, I was confused as to what that statement was. I somehow felt vindicated and began to feel very smug that nobody was sleeping now. Although I knew full well God was the One doing the healing, pride had crept in because He was using me as the vessel to bring it.

I went to the next person to be prayed for, knowing he was going to get healed no matter what. I will call him "Pete." Pete said he always had pain in his feet but didn't say why. I knelt down in front of him and was about to start praying when I heard the Holy Spirit tell me, "Stand up, and do not pray for him." I could tell by the tone in His voice some type of rebuke was coming.

This was not the first time I had seen the Holy Spirit do this while I was ministering. There had been other times when this had happened, and the Holy Spirit would then give me a word of knowledge about something in the person's life that needed to be dealt with or corrected before I was to pray for their original concern. At that point I would lean forward and whisper in the individual's ear about the situation or take him or her off to the side for privacy.

I stood back waiting for the message, anticipating that this young man was about to get corrected by the Lord for some reason. To my surprise, when the Holy Spirit spoke, it was not a word of correction for the young man. It was a word of correction for me!

He simply said, "This is not the Bruce show. This is My show, and you will not pray for another person standing up here. I am going to continue to do miracles but not through you. Pick others out of the crowd to do the praying."

I felt sick to my stomach as I realized how easily I had been sucked into pride after foolishly feeling insulted by the sleepers.

I made the statement to the crowd that the Lord was going to heal everyone who had been called up for prayer and then asked for volunteers to do the praying. At first no one wanted to, but I began to explain how the pressure was not on us but on God. I told them that none of us have the ability to heal anyone in and of ourselves. I then began to do some basic teaching on how to pray for people before I asked for volunteers again. I explained that they could and should pray for their family and friends and expect God to hear and answer wherever they were, not because of them but because of His faithfulness. Our sovereign God tells us to pray for others; therefore, the results are out of our control. There is no pressure on us except to believe with the faith of a mustard seed.

When I asked who would like to pray for Pete and his feet, a tall youth raised his hand near the front, and I motioned him forward through the crowd. I coached him quickly again on how I would pray and turned him loose.

After he prayed, we asked Pete to test his feet out. He stood up and walked around a bit and soberly said the pain was now gone. Several months later Pete contacted me and told me the rest of the story. Pete had been born with flat feet. He had no arches in his feet, and because of that, his feet hurt whenever he was on them. When his father had come to pick him up later that day from the camp, one of the pastors cautiously mentioned Pete felt the Lord had healed his feet earlier that morning at our meeting. The father replied, "That's simple to find out—either he now has arches or he doesn't." He told his son to take off his shoes and socks. To the surprise of the pastor and the father Pete had perfect arches.

Pete's story doesn't end there. His mother's leg had been operated on the previous year, and it had never healed right, causing her great pain. After Pete got home, he kept thinking of how the Lord had healed him and how I had encouraged them not to be afraid to pray for family members. After some time of struggling with the idea, he decided he would give it a try, and he laid hands on his mother and prayed over her leg. The Lord instantly healed his mother. It made such an impact on Pete that he decided to go into full-time ministry upon graduating.

That day at the camp we saw the Lord perform many astounding healings and miracles, from the ones I mentioned already to several others. After all the people who had been called out were prayed for and healed, many other people also came forward for prayer and were healed, including a girl who had badly damaged her intestines because of a severe eating disorder. I never got to finish telling my complete testimony, but obviously that wasn't what God had planned that day. As it turned out, to my knowledge, every single person who ended up getting prayed for was healed that day except for two, one of the pastors and his child who had requested that I personally pray for them at the very end of the service.

As I travel around the country ministering, I will often say that I preach on my own shortcomings and downfalls so that I never run out of material. The group always gets a big laugh out of that statement, but it is the truth, and this story proves it. Thank God for His grace and mercy.

I felt led to start the book with this testimony for several reasons.

1. It proves God can and will use imperfect people to accomplish His will despite our mistakes or feelings of inadequacy.

2. It shows that if we are connected and obedient to the Lord, He will give us every tool we need for victory in life, regardless of the circumstances. Our trials can become opportunities for God's light to shine when we invite Him into the situation.

3. It demonstrates God wants to use all of us to be His hands and His feet. When we make ourselves available, He will not only bless our efforts, but also He will multiply them, causing a snowball effect that will continue to grow beyond what we could ever imagine.

As you read this book, may the Lord cement these truths in your heart and mind so you can live a miraculous life of victory and see other people saved, healed, and delivered as well!

Part One

The Five Main Miracles That Have Shaped My Life

Part One

The Five Main Miracles That
Have Shaped My Life

E ACH ONE OF US is going to face situations, "giants" if you will, of adversity in our lives. Some are bigger than others. But regardless of the size or the source, sooner or later they are going to come.

When the inevitable problems of this life arise, God wants us to be able to come out on the other side of those problems more mature and complete than before. Many people would agree that when looked back upon, the biggest struggles in their lives actually became defining moments that changed who they were forever.

It is our choice if a problem is going to make us *bitter* or *better*, and our attitude will determine that. If given the chance, God loves to turn around hopeless situations and make them into opportunities to accomplish His will in our lives.

To be fair, things don't always turn out as we want or even suspect. But when we turn over a situation to the Lord, we can trust Him. We can believe that He is not only going to give us the weapons we need to fight with, but He is also going to make it turn out for good in the long run. *God delights in turning the disastrous into the miraculous when invited into a situation!*

The next five chapters start out by examining some of the astounding miracles that have shaped my life. All of these miracles were birthed in the midst of suffering, heartache, and grief, bringing good from bad—such as being hugged by Jesus at age five after being molested, God calling my name in a church service because of drug addiction, being rescued from death by two angels the Lord sent to save my life, the Holy Spirit coming into my bedroom as a very strong wind and calming my overwhelming fear, and Jesus appearing to me and commissioning me while in the midst of discouragement. Each one of these miraculous encounters revealed to me knowledge and insight I will share with you, all within the context of Scripture.

We see over and over in the Bible where the Lord would do this same thing, taking a seemingly hopeless situation and turning it around into a testimony of His love, power, and faithfulness. One of the most prominent illustrations of that is the account of David and Goliath. Throughout this book we will see how this testimony gives us godly wisdom and hope for our lives today.

Before David was the great and all-powerful king of Israel, he was a shepherd boy and the runt of his family. Even after the prophet Samuel anointed him, he was not able to come into his God-given destiny until he faced some "giants." His first battles were with wild animals, and what he learned from those encounters helped give him the faith in God he needed to overcome a foe who was bigger, meaner, stronger, and smarter. We too have a God-ordained destiny, and like David we are going to have to go through different battles in this life before we can be who God has called us to be.

I have heard it said before that you have to go through the "test" in order to get a "testimony." Our spiritual maturity happens not in spite of our hardships, but most often because of them. In case you missed that foundational truth, let me repeat it. Our spiritual maturity happens not in spite of our hardships, but most often because of them. Please don't misunderstand me, I am not a sadistic person who thinks we should go out chasing trouble, but I believe we can't ignore what the Bible tells us. James 1:2–4 says, "Consider it pure joy, my brothers, whenever you face trials of many kinds, because you know that the testing of your faith develops perseverance. Perseverance must finish its work so that you may be mature and complete, not lacking anything."

When we can maintain a right attitude and continue to be obedient to God despite a seemingly hopeless situation or hardship, it will build courage, authority, and character in us that will help us become the champions we were meant to be. That's the reason James could say, "Consider it pure joy," because he knew the outcome would be greater than the ordeal!

My hope and prayer for you is that after reading the next five chapters, you will be able to realize the different times and ways the Lord has worked to bring good from the bad in your own life, or the lives of others, and how you are a better person today because of it. If you can't see that any good has come from a trial you have encountered, I pray you would ask God to show you what it was in case you missed it. You can also pray and ask Him to intervene in the situation, then wait and see what He is going to do as it is never too late.

Romans 8:28 says, "And we know that in all things God works for the good of those who love him, who have been called according to his purpose." He is faithful and His promises are true. Believing God's Word above our circumstances is not always easy, but when we do it, we will see His promises to us fulfilled.

Chapter 1

Hugged by Jesus

AS A YOUNG child I grew up in a home where we did not attend church regularly. Although both of my parents believed in God, I did not come from a "religious" or "churchy" home by any means. In fact, oftentimes it was quite contrary to that. I think it is important to preface the story I am about to tell you with these facts so that you understand this miraculous encounter didn't happen in some fanatically religious home but one that was bruised and struggling—as many are today.

My father was a long-distance truck driver. My mother also worked out of the home, which meant there were times I had to stay with another family. Sometimes they would watch me overnight. It was during these stays when bad things began to happen to me at around the age of five years.

These people were "party" people as my parents were, but they were also very heavy into pornography. I clearly remember stacks of pornographic magazines lying around the house as well as pornographic movies that they would play on the wall of their living room with an old reel-to-reel movie projector.

The mother and father of this family would get drunk and then start watching these movies while their own two children and I were in the room. Sometimes they would get sexual with each other in front of us, and if this weren't bad enough already, periodically they would involve us children in their perversion.

I am not exactly sure how it is possible, but oftentimes children who get molested are manipulated into not telling anyone. This was the case for me. Over the course of the next year the molestation continued without me saying a word to anyone.

God Plants His Word

It was during that time that my grandpa and grandma ended up watching me on a weekend for some reason. While I was staying at their house, they took me to church with them and I attended Sunday school for the first and only time I can remember as a child. The year would have been somewhere around 1975.

The church was very small and old, located in a rural area close to where my grandparents lived. When it was time for Sunday school, I remember clearly that a man in a brown polyester suit with long pointy collars led the few children who were there into the basement to a small table for the class. I recall feeling very nervous. The man must have been able to tell this because he sat me right next to himself and kept patting me on the back.

He handed out a coloring sheet to each of us so we could color it in with crayons. The picture was of a bearded man holding children in his arms. He said the man was Jesus. Then he read the story to us from the Bible where Jesus blesses and holds the children despite the complaints from His disciples. (See Mark 10:13–16.) The Sunday school teacher told us that this story proved Jesus loved children and if we prayed to Him, He would hear us and answer us.

I remember being confused. Although I didn't believe this story, I could tell this nice man in the "odd" clothes did. Months passed before I ever thought about this subject again.

The Hands of God

One day some people had come to visit at our house, and I was caught exhibiting some sexual behavior with one of the visiting children. My mother was appalled and asked me where I had learned such things. Unfortunately the threats, lies, and manipulation of the adults who were molesting me were strong enough to get me to not tell my mother the truth. Instead I said it was the babysitters' son who had shown me these things. This boy who was only a few years older than me was being molested just as I was at his house, but for some reason I blamed him instead of his parents.

My father was not home at the time. My mother said that when he got home, I was going to have to tell him what I had been caught doing. I could tell my mother was very upset. Though I was only five, I knew deep inside that the things going on at the babysitters' house and what I had just done were very, very wrong.

The day finally came when my dad was supposed to come home from his current trip. After supper my mother sat me on top of their bed and told me at some point she was going to come and get me so I could tell my dad what I had been caught doing. I heard my dad come in and listened through the closed door to my parents as they talked.

It is hard to explain how dirty and bad I felt as I lay there on their bed, waiting for punishment. I believed everything that had happened was all my fault and that I must be a very bad person. Lying there in the dark, I started to cry as the grief and weight of the whole situation began to feel unbearable. I wanted so badly to be held and comforted, but it was clear this was not going to happen.

In the midst of this fear and inner pain a thought came into my mind. It reminded me of what the Sunday school teacher had said months before, that if we would pray to Jesus, He would hear our prayer and answer because of His love for us.

I decided I had nothing to lose, so I prayed a very simple prayer.

I said, "Jesus, if You are real, I want You to come and give me a hug right now." Immediately Someone sat me up on the bed and wrapped their arms around me. A light came into the dark room that seemed to be only where I was. I could physically feel arms holding me and a chest I leaned on, but I couldn't see anyone.

Instantly the most incredible sensation of love unimaginable engulfed me. Mere words can't accurately describe what happened that night. It was as if my body had been dipped in liquid love from the top of my head to the bottom of my feet. I was covered by this warm presence of love. This sensation was very physical, yet somehow this "liquid love" had also gone right to the very center of my being.

The sorrow, grief, and pain I had been feeling was completely gone. A perfect peace replaced those feelings, and the only thing I felt on the inside was the same intense love I felt on the outside. My physical and emotional perceptions had melted into one giant ball of love, and I drifted off into a deep sleep.

The next morning I woke up still dressed from the day before and still on top of my parents' bed. My parents had not come and gotten me for our talk. They had not even come to bed that night.

I remember replaying the events of the night before in my head and coming to a very quick conclusion. There is something to this "Jesus" thing! Although I never told a soul what happened that night for more than twenty years, it cemented in my mind the absolute truth of the reality of Jesus.

New Experiences

Right after this first supernatural encounter with God occurred, some other extraordinary things began to happen. One night I had a very intense dream, one so vivid that even now, more than thirty-five years later, I can still remember parts of it. In this dream I was walking hand in hand with Jesus down a road made of strange material in a place I had never seen before. On each side of the road were tall walls made out the most amazing stones you could imagine. They were all different colors and seemed to glisten and gleam no matter how you looked at them. Jesus never spoke in the dream, but I somehow knew it was Him and we were walking in heaven.

I remember telling my mother about the dream and her getting scared because she thought maybe it was a sign something bad was going to happen to me. She knew what I had described in my dream was the way the Bible describes heaven. She also knew there was no way I would or should have known that. The dream hadn't scared me at all because while walking with Jesus in the dream, I again experienced great peace and joy.

I began to periodically have prophetic dreams and visions also. Sometimes I would see a picture in my head, or I would have a dream at night about something happening in real life. Later the dream would come true, right down to the small details that weren't even important. I remember the first time this happened and how shocked I was as I watched it play out.

My father's pickup truck had broken down in my dream, and a man I had never met or seen before came over to our house to help him work on it. A few days after having the dream, my dad's truck did break down, and he brought it into our barn so he could fix it. I went into the musty barn and sat down, watching my dad work on the old black Chevy.

As I was sitting there, I realized I had dreamed this exact scene just days earlier. Right on cue, the man from my dream who had helped my dad walked into the barn that night and put his right foot up on the front bumper of the truck before saying a sarcastic comment, just as he had done in my dream. It turned out this man was someone my dad worked with at his job, and he had decided to stop by and see if he could help.

In addition to these dreams I now began to sense and sometimes even "see" things in the spirit realm. As a child I didn't understand why I sensed or felt these things and would very often just try to ignore them. To be honest, there were times I saw things that terrified me to the point I wished I didn't have these encounters at all. I learned later this was called spiritual discernment.

From Victim to Victory

Being repeatedly molested as a small child and feeling like everything that happened was all my fault was a miserable experience for me. The things that happened and even the things it caused me to do were very unfortunate, but I can now see how God was able to take this tragedy and turn it into something glorious.

God used my grandparents to take me to a Sunday school teacher who then planted the seed of God's Word in my heart so that when it seemed as though nothing could get any worse in my life, I would know that I could call out to Him. When I did, He poured out His love on me in such a magnificent way that my life would be changed forever.

No matter what has ever happened to me since, or what will ever happen in the future, I know that I know that I know Jesus is real, and so is His love! This is a priceless gift in and of itself, but God didn't stop there.

When He came and hugged me that night, it was more than just a hug. We read in the Bible many places where God's servants had hands laid on them to receive an anointing or impartation of His presence that always ended up manifesting in some type of spiritual gifting (Num. 27:23; Deut. 34:9; Acts 6:6; 13:3).

This explains why after having "holy hands" put on me I began to have prophetic dreams and visions as well as have my spiritual eyes opened. Although I might not have liked some of the things that came with this as a child, now that I am older I can see just how beneficial these gifts are in ministry and in my personal walk with the Lord.

The other very significant thing that this encounter did for me was that it made me appreciate just how important it is for us to realize how much God loves us. In fact, I believe it is probably the most important thing we need to know in order to have a healthy relationship with God. First John 4:19 reads, "We love because he first loved us."

If we don't believe or grasp how much God loves us, how could we ever really even begin to trust Him or want to have a close relationship with Him? That is why this is such a foundational truth that needs to be deeply imbedded in the heart of every believer.

The Reality of God's Love

I have seen people so hurt by life that no matter how many times they were told of God's love, they just couldn't accept it. For these people I pray that God would supernaturally make His love known to them as only He can do. I have witnessed people who were very desperate for a touch from God call out to Him in deep desperation and receive their own supernatural experience after hearing my testimony of getting hugged by Jesus as a child.

One woman related that her husband was an atheist who was dying of cancer, so she bought my book *Saved by Angels* for him to read. When he read about Jesus hugging me as a child, he called out to God with all his heart, saying, "If You are real, then I need You to touch me too." Then something that looked like a bolt of lightning came into the room and zapped him. She was in another room of the house, not aware of what he had just prayed, but she saw this flash of bright light and ran into the room he was in to see what had happened. He was crying and told her what he had just prayed and what he experienced in his heart when the flash of light—love and power—hit him. Needless to say, he accepted Jesus as his Lord and Savior that day.

The Lord has given me many dreams and visions that pertain to His great love for us. I could relate several stories just like this that prove it over and over.

There have been many times while praying over people and

ministering to them that the Lord has had me pray that the person or even whole church would be dipped in His liquid love, just as I had experienced that night long ago. All people need to feel loved by others, and to know that God loves us is even more important than that.

Several times we have seen where a person just can't seem to get healed, delivered, or set free. The Holy Spirit ends up giving a word of knowledge that the person doesn't believe God can or does love them. After talking and praying through that issue until the person is able to believe it, we will very often then see an immediate answer to their original prayer.

Late one night at a church after giving my testimony and praying over people for hours, a little girl walked up to the pastor of the church and me as we were discussing the night's events. She was a fiery little six- or seven-year-old redhead who had been born with problems in her intestines that caused her pain and digestion issues on a daily basis.

She pointed her finger at me and said she had heard me say earlier in the evening "more than once" that when we prayed to Jesus, He would hear us and answer us. She then reminded me I had prayed for the pain in her stomach to go away three times that night, but she still had it. With a scowl on her face she proceeded to stare at me in uncomfortable silence, at which point the pastor got up and walked away, leaving me to deal with the thorny problem I had seemingly created.

I asked her if I could pray for her one more time, and after rolling her eyes, she reluctantly said yes. As I knelt before her, I silently asked God what He wanted me to do or even say. Immediately I felt His great love for her and His sorrow over the situation to the point I began to weep uncontrollably. The Holy Spirit then told me to tell her that she could trust God because He loved her, so I did. After finishing, He told me to say it again. Over and over the cycle repeated itself until unexpectantly the power of God hit her and she fell to the floor seemingly unconscious.

I continued to pray and asked the Lord to give me understanding in the situation. He reminded me this girl was raised in a Christian home and had heard her mom and dad pray for her stomach many times, but the pain had never left and she had never been healed.

Somewhere in this child's mind she had therefore concluded that God must not really love her that much and He could not be completely trusted to come through when it counted. Now He was doing a work inside of her heart to remove those doubts and replace them with His love while she was lying on the floor at the front of the church.

After a while her mother got a little nervous and began to try and wake her up, but one of the elders from the church encouraged her to just let God keep doing whatever He was doing. About ten minutes later the little girl came to and asked what had happened. These people didn't attend this particular church, and I am sure this girl had never seen someone get slain in the Spirit before that night.

I found out later that although her stomach did improve greatly, it is not completely healed yet. That is actually one of the main reasons I felt led to share this particular story. I could relate to you many, many testimonies that after the person accepted and received the immense love that God had for them, they were completely healed of their physical or emotional problem, but I am trying to make another point here. After Jesus hugged me that night and I went out under the power and love, it did not change the fact that I had been molested. I still had to deal with the repercussions of that for several years. What it did change, though, was even more important than that. It showed me God was real and He does love us regardless of what happens or how we feel. This little redhead learned as I did that we can trust Him to always be there for us, no matter what.

Good From Bad

Jesus said that the devil comes to steal, kill, and destroy, but that He came that we might have life and have it to the full or more abundantly (John 10:10). These testimonies show what that looks like in daily living. One of the struggles we are going to have in this life is with other humans. The work of the enemy caused me to be molested by evil people, but God used a promise from His Word to turn the whole situation around so that in the end incredible good would come out of it—not just good for me, but also good for others as they hear what happened and contemplate what it means for their own life, like the ex-atheist who was hit with a bolt of lightning from God when he called out to Him and the little girl who learned she could trust God no matter how her stomach felt.

God will bring good from bad when we invite Him into a situation. The good will then grow and multiply as we share it with others.

Only He can do that, and He wants to do it not only in my life but in your life as well. There is never a situation too bad, too far gone, or too old for God to step in and turn things around when we call on Him. This is what Jesus was sent to do. First John 3:8 says, "The reason the Son of God appeared was to destroy the devil's work."

Chapter 2

When God Called My Name

A FTER GETTING HUGGED by Jesus as a child, the knowledge that God would hear us when we cried out to Him never left me. Unfortunately at the time I didn't realize this was true of day-to-day life and that He wanted a constant relationship with me, so I relegated praying to Him for times of crisis only.

He became a "911" God who I believed could be called upon only when there was something really bad going on. (Sadly there are many "Christians" around the world today who have fallen into this same trap.) Because of this, from the time I was hugged by Jesus until I was in high school, I had only prayed to Him genuinely, or sincerely, a small number of times.

Each time I did pray He always answered, proving His faithfulness. For example, when I was about fourteen years old one of my younger brothers got cancer and wasn't expected to live. One day instead of going to the hospital to visit him, I stayed home and earnestly prayed for a few hours asking the Lord to heal him. Within a day or two of praying, everything started to turn around, and my brother ended up fully recovering. I knew that this was a result of God intervening.

Because of being molested and other things that happened in my childhood, I carried around a lot of pain on the inside, as many people do. In order to deal with this pain, I began to smoke pot about the time I started high school. I became instantly addicted because it was a way for me to escape reality and numb the bad feelings I had in my heart.

Addiction Begins

Before long I was smoking pot from the time I got up in the morning until I went to bed at night. In order to be able to afford my habit and to ensure I always had some, I began selling it also. This opened the door for me to begin to experiment with many other different kinds of drugs and become involved with a lot of hurting people who were also heading the wrong direction in life.

During that time I was drawn to a girl I went to high school with who was very different from me. We began to date, and I felt that another person really loved me for the first time in my life. She came from a very stable and loving Christian family that was almost dreamlike to me. I couldn't get enough of going to her house and hanging out with her family so I could try to soak in what they had.

Despite this, my drug addiction continued to grow. I was regularly doing other drugs and drinking alcohol at times in addition to my daily marijuana use.

I ended up asking this girl to marry me just after we graduated from high school. She said yes, but things quickly unraveled. One weekend shortly after we became engaged, I made the several hours drive to see her at college and found out that her parents were not happy with the engagement at all.

They told her if she planned on marrying me, they were going to quit paying for her college education and would no longer support her or the marriage in any way. They were so against the marriage it sounded as if they would disown her if she decided to marry me.

She said it all came down to my substance abuse. They had found out I did drugs as well as sold them and didn't want their daughter mixed up with those things. She said if I agreed to quit and would completely change my lifestyle, maybe her parents would relent.

I instantly felt rejected. I told her that if she or her parents couldn't accept me for who I was, then we shouldn't get married. At the time I was far too selfish and deep into addiction to think rationally about the situation or anyone else's point of view. In my mind drug use wasn't optional; it was survival, a way of life, and I was so bound up in it I didn't think I could live without it. I believed that if she couldn't accept me the way I was, then she must not really love me.

We fought all afternoon. I had planned on spending the night, but I was tired of arguing and began to walk to the parking lot so I could leave. She begged me to stay, but I didn't want to fight any more. I felt betrayed by her and her family. My thinking was misguided, but it still hurt very much. I had some high-grade pot in my car, and all I could think about was smoking some so I could push this whole mess right off my mind. The feeling of being comfortably numb was calling me, and I was ready.

God Makes the Call

As we stood next to the car, my girlfriend said she would make me a deal. If I would go to church with her in the morning, she would drop the conversation and we could move on as if nothing had ever happened. After church I could leave and we would go our separate ways if that's what I chose, or if I decided to quit using drugs, I could stay and we could make things work out.

I agreed to her deal and decided that after church I was going to leave and our relationship would be over, fully believing it wasn't my choice but hers.

The next morning as we walked to the church in awkward silence, something strange happened. We were on the sidewalk about one hundred yards from the church when I began to feel a very strong presence of the Lord. I immediately recognized it was Him from the past encounters I had experienced, but this time something was different.

I felt His love as I had in the past, but there was also a strong sense of conviction that came with it this time. With every step we took closer to the church, the overwhelming sense of His divine presence increased. It felt as if every hair on my body was standing on end, and finally I stopped walking, unable to go on.

Standing there on the sidewalk I felt emotionally and spiritually naked before an all-knowing, all-powerful God.

My girlfriend asked me what was the matter. I told her I had changed my mind; I didn't want to go to church with her, and I was leaving right now. She reminded me about our deal and my promise. I started to turn and leave, but she grabbed my hand and pulled with all her might, telling me I could leave right after church.

She somehow convinced me to go in with her. I was very uncomfortable and even borderline fearful of what might happen in there. I can remember exactly where we sat that morning. It was in the second to last row in the church not far from the exit. (I would have chosen the very back row right next to the door, but it had already been taken.)

The service started with some announcements. Then we sang a song from a small booklet that had praise songs in it as well as hymns. I don't remember what the song was, but I do remember it described the condition of my heart and the sin that was so deep in my life. It was as if the song was written just for me at that exact moment in my journey on life's path. As I sang the song from the bottom of my heart, something supernatural began to happen. The intense presence of God seemed to be hovering right over me. It was clear that I needed to make a choice between right and wrong, good and bad.

Thoughts began to race through my mind almost faster than I could keep up with them. Systematically each one of my arguments trying to justify my drug use were broken down and shown to me as what they were—lies I believed and excuses I used.

It was as if someone had unzipped my chest and handed me my heart after showing me everything that was wrong with it.

The song ended and a hymn began. My eyes were following along with the words on the page, but my heart was still contemplating how the last song was so true. That's when it happened. God called out my name in that church so loud I thought the building was going to collapse. It wasn't like a yell, yet it was so powerful and loud the earth itself seemed to tremble. (I found later that the Bible describes this in Psalm 29:4–5 where it says that the voice of the Lord is so powerful and majestic it can break trees into pieces.)

When it happened, I jumped up in the air like a startled cat, and the booklet flew out of my hand. I turned around and looked at all the people in the back row, as it seemed like the voice came from right behind me. People were still singing, and only the few people who were directly in back of me had stopped to look at me. I could tell by the look in their eyes they were puzzled by my actions and thought I was some kind of crazy weirdo.

As impossible as it seemed, I realized I was the only one who had heard my name called out. What was even more incredible was the fact that although I heard only my name, somehow much more than that had been spoken to me.

I have heard it said that a picture can say a thousand words. That is a good analogy for what happened to me that day. Just one word from God instantly downloaded a thousand messages into my heart.

His calling out my name communicated, "Bruce, I love you. I want the best for you. Come to Me, and I can give you peace. I can remove your pain. You're believing lies, but I have the truth. You're making bad choices, and you're going the wrong direction. The path you're on leads to sorrow and danger. Follow Me instead."

I somehow knew He had whispered these same messages to my heart many times before throughout the years. But then He said something that completely took me by surprise. He was calling me into full-time ministry. My job, my occupation, was to be working for Him. Someone had just offered to help pay my way through college, and He wanted me to use that opportunity to go to Bible college instead of the tech school I was looking at.

Wrong Choices

I could believe God loved me and could understand I was going the wrong direction in life, but it was too much to think I was supposed to be in ministry. Had He forgotten where I came from or what kind of person I was? I knew I was a sinner who wasn't worthy of His love. I also believed I surely wasn't the kind of person who should be telling anybody about a holy God.

I got out of that church as quick as I could that day and almost ran to my vehicle. Although I wasn't happy my relationship with that girl was officially over, I was happy the church service was. After getting out on the highway, I began to smoke the high-powered marijuana I had hidden in my car. After being a daily user for years, my tolerances were built up pretty far, and it took "good weed" like this to even get me high.

On the long car ride home I kept smoking puff after puff until I was so high I was having a hard time even keeping my eyes open. Over and over I told myself, "That did not just happen. God did not just call my name." But no matter how much I smoked, I couldn't make the memory of it go away. I knew in my heart of hearts it had happened and it was real, but I didn't want to believe it.

That day I ran away from God when He called me as Jonah did in the Bible, and just like Jonah I ran right into the belly of a whale, only mine didn't spit me up on the shore after three days as his did (Jon. 1–2). My display of free will kept me in the bowels of addiction, depression, and agony for another sixteen years.

The hardest part of sharing this story is admitting that even though God did a miracle by showing up and literally telling me which way to go, I still went the wrong direction. I chose not to listen, and because of it I hindered what He wanted to do for me and with me at that point in my life.

Maybe you can relate to this and know what it is like to blow it even after God or someone He sent tried to guide you down the right path. We all are going to make choices and decisions we will regret at some point in our lives. But thank the Lord for His forgiveness, mercy, and grace.

How many times have we heard someone say if only they knew then what they know now, they would have made a different choice?

If I would have known that day that just two years later I was going to suffer a severe cocaine overdose; that I would end up wasting so much time, effort, and money on drugs; or that they would end up making me miserable, it would have helped me make the right choice. I didn't know these things, but God did and He tried to warn me. I chose not to listen and ended up paying quite a price for it over the next several years.

God does want the best for us. He will do miracles and step into our lives, but He still gives us free will to make our own choices.

We see this same principle at work over and over in the Bible as well. When God parted the Red Sea, the Israelites had to step into it to be saved (Exod. 14). When God made the walls of Jericho fall down, the Israelites still had to go into the city and fight to obtain it (Josh. 6). When Jesus died, the veil was torn in the earthly temple, representing the removal of the barrier between God and man (Matt. 27). Jesus's death made a way for all people to have relationship with God. However, we still have to choose to enter into a relationship with Him before we can be eternally saved. This is probably the most important example of all.

God's Redeeming Character

Our God is a God of mercy and grace, and He has a way of redeeming the lost years in our lives.

Although I had run away from what He wanted me to do that day, I was never able to run away from His presence or the call He had on my life. His purposes stand throughout the ages, and over time He continued to draw me closer and closer to Him and even began to use me to carry out His will in other people's lives despite the addictions I struggled with.

One night at the age of twenty-three I prayed for the Lord to send me a soul mate and companion who would love me even though I was addicted to drugs and felt like a complete looser. The very next day the Lord supernaturally pointed Lori out to me in a crowd by making her appear literally to be glowing. We began dating, and within a few months she ended up receiving Jesus into her heart after I told her how He had hugged me when I called out to Him as a five-year-old. She was the very first person I ever told what happened to me that night as a child, and I was shocked at the impact it had on her.

We ended up getting married a year later, and because of the radical change that took place in her life after accepting Jesus, we started to attend church regularly. Throughout the following decade God used married life, having children, and regular church attendance to greatly impact the direction of my life.

After many years of healing me on the inside and getting me to a place where I could do the things He wanted me to do, one of the last things that stood in the way was this nagging addiction to drugs and alcohol.

I no longer sold drugs, and I got to the point where I didn't have to do them all day long. I could wait to smoke until I got home from work and no longer had to carry some with me wherever I went. I quit doing all other drugs except pot and the occasional use of alcohol or cocaine, but those became rare too. Before long I was able to even skip a day here or there. It was about then that I really began to call out to God to set me free from this addiction once and for all.

I would get high and then feel so guilty I would flush my pot down the toilet and ask God to forgive me. I would promise Him I would never do it again but turn right around and go buy more a few days later. Although the periods of time between using kept increasing, this gut-wrenching cycle went on for a few years. I came to the point where I knew that if I was ever going to get set free from drugs, God was going to have to supernaturally do it.

Around that time my pastor invited me to come and listen to some people who were doing short-term missions work in Africa. After hearing their story, my wife and I ended up giving them a van we had for sale. When the husband-and-wife team came to pick it up at our house, they thanked us profusely and asked if we had any prayer requests.

I answered that I had been addicted to drugs and alcohol for over twenty years and would like prayer for that. Although I did not know these people at all and they weren't from our town, the wife began to tell me about my past. She told me I had been molested as a child and even about how old I was when it happened, as well as some other things. The Lord was giving her words of knowledge about me that nobody would have known, and it got my attention in a hurry.

She ended by saying that my addiction issues were not physical in origin as I had supposed, but they were spiritual in nature and had actually been with me since I had been molested as a child. After she and her husband prayed over my wife and me, I was completely set free from drugs and alcohol right on the spot.

Although I struggled with addiction much longer than I needed to and had passed up the opportunity for God to miraculously remove my addictions sixteen years earlier that day in the church, He brought it to pass anyway and was even able to use it for good in the end.

Now that the addiction issues were out of the way, ministry began to really take off in my life. Because of living in addiction so long myself, I was able to minister quite effectively to others who were also bound up in addictions of various types. God used the long drawn-out struggle I went through to help others in their own battles. Sometimes the trials we face are not quickly over, and we need to learn to persevere so that we can become mature and complete as the Bible says in James 1:2–4.

There were several times when people with addictions wouldn't listen or receive what a pastor or counselor was telling them about God, but they would listen to me because I had been through it and could relate to them and their struggles. God was able to turn around what the enemy had meant to destroy me and use it for the good of many people.

I began to lead more Bible studies at church and at our home, and we saw God do amazing things in people's lives. The Lord then opened doors for me to speak in front of our congregation a few times. I was very nervous to be up front speaking, but people began to tell me that I should be a preacher.

One of the pastors from our church, Ryan Clark, had become a good friend of mine. He had recently left our church and took a call to be a pastor of a church in New York. One day while I was talking to him on the phone, he said that the Lord had just told him I was to be an evangelist. I got off the phone and went outside of the garage I was working at that day in my diesel repair business and lay down prostrate on the ground and began to pray. I told the Lord if he wanted me to be an evangelist, He was going to have to tell me and not Pastor Ryan.

Immediately the Lord told me to get up off the ground and quit praying. I was supposed to go back in the garage and write down all the times He had already told me but I hadn't listened. I went in the garage and filled up nearly two notebook pages of times and ways He had called me into ministry, with the very first one being the day He called my name in that church.

God had not only wanted to set me free from addictions that day so long ago, but He had also called me into full-time ministry. Even though I hadn't been obedient, He hadn't changed His mind.

As I began to turn toward God, the miracle of Him calling my name that day in the church as we were singing His praises was carrying out what He had planned it to do, despite my failures and mistakes.

God has plans for each one of us, and that includes you. Jeremiah 29:11 says, "'For I know the plans I have for you,' declares the LORD, 'plans to prosper you and not to harm you, plans to give you a hope and a future.'"

God spoke these words to His people after they had made some big mistakes and had suffered several years because of their disobedience. If you are in a place where you too have suffered for several years in one way or another, either from your own fault or not, then know this: God is a God who can and will redeem us and our mistakes, even the mistakes of others in our lives, when we turn our hearts to Him.

Chapter 3

Saved by God's Angels

IN JULY OF 2006 we planned on driving from where we lived in Wisconsin out to New York so we could go visit Pastor Ryan and his family.

Sometime before we left, I had a dream one night that I knew was from God, although I didn't find out entirely what it meant for almost two years.

In the dream I was in a line of people who were walking down a path. We came to a blue pickup truck, and a faceless man (this always represents the Holy Spirit in my dreams) was in the bed handing out bread to people. The pickup bed was filled to overflowing with round platters of every imaginable type of bread you could think of. Each person would walk up and point to the platter they wanted, and the faceless man would then hand it to them. After receiving the platter of bread, the people entered a large open-air pavilion that had rows of wooden picnic tables and would sit down to eat.

When it was my turn, I looked over all the choices searching for some sweet bread and realized there was only one platter like it in the truck, so I happily chose it. The bread was a honey yellow color and had frosting on top with swirls of cinnamon and raisins in it as well.

As I was eating my sweet bread, I watched as a tall bearded man came through the line past the truck. After looking over all the choices, he walked on without taking one. No one else had done this! He began to go up and down the tables looking at each person's platter. When he got to mine, he stopped, apparently finding what he was looking for.

Without saying a word, he reached down and took a piece of sweet bread from my platter and began to eat it. I didn't say anything to him but was a little annoyed by this as he had the chance to get his own bread but didn't. I quickly finished eating the piece in my hand and grabbed another one from the platter. He did the same. Again I was a little bothered by it, but we were both enjoying how good it tasted, and there seemed to be enough for both of us. I looked around and realized that many other people were now eyeing up the sweet bread, and I became afraid I would have to share the sweet bread with them too.

In my dream, God then spoke to my heart and asked me if I had done something to get the bread or if it was a gift. I replied that it was a gift. He said, "Because it was a gift, you should be happy to share it." I woke up and immediately prayed for the interpretation of the dream, but the only thing the Lord told me was that it had to do with Pastor Ryan.

The next morning I called Pastor Ryan and told him the dream from beginning to end. I asked him what he thought it meant. He joked and said maybe I went to bed hungry or something. He had no idea what it could mean.

Prophecy Speaks

A few weeks passed, and we drove out to New York for our vacation. While we were visiting his new church, Pastor Ryan introduced us to ministry friends, members of his church, and others he had gotten to know since he became pastor. To my surprise up walked the bearded man from my sweet bread dream! He was even dressed in the exact same clothes I had seen in the dream.

The man's name was Bruce Carlson, and he worked at the church full-time as a worship leader/teacher/evangelist. I told him about the dream, and Ryan confirmed what I had described on the phone before we left, including the clothing. We were all surprised by this strange occurrence, as there didn't seem to be any real reason for the Lord to have given the dream at this point. Only time would tell what it really meant and just how prophetic it was.

While we were still in New York, Ryan invited me to a pastor's prayer meeting he attended weekly. During the meeting Ralph Diaz, a pastor who is known for having a strong prophetic gifting, said the Lord had given him some words for me. One of the things he said was that I was going to start a powerful ministry and that the glory of the Lord would surround the ministry and me. He also said I would be seeing angels very soon, and that while I was there on vacation, I would meet someone who would be very important in my future.

We drove back home after our vacation was over and resumed normal life once again. I jotted these seemingly odd occurrences down in my journal and didn't give them a whole lot more thought as my diesel repair business kept me very busy working lots of hours.

The Question

During that summer the Holy Spirit began to ask me a troubling question from time to time. He kept asking me if I would die for the advancement of the kingdom. The question made me very uncomfortable, so when it came I would ignore it, as if I hadn't heard it. (Those of you who are married or have children might have seen this tactic used before.)

This question was so far out of the norm that I was very hesitant to even mention it to anyone. Eventually I called Pastor Ryan and told him what had been happening. His response caught me off guard. He said he knew how on fire I was for God and that I must have said yes.

Pastor Ryan's words made me feel very convicted for refusing to answer God when He had asked me the question. I continued to ponder the subject but could never get any peace about it or an answer I was comfortable with.

As strange as this might sound to some people, one of the best places for me to have conversations with God at times is in the shower. There are no telephones, radios, TVs, or computers to distract me. My wife, children, and even the dog leave me alone in the shower. I can have dialogue with God and even sing praises to Him without having to feel self-conscious about what I say or how I sound. I do not have to deal with any distractions either. It has been a refuge of intimacy for me to spend quality time with the Lord throughout the years.

It was during one of these shower conversations with God that He asked me the question again: "Would you die for the advancement of the kingdom?" This time was different, though, because the Holy Spirit then said I couldn't get out of the shower until I answered, as I had all summer to think about it already.

We had built our house, and with six people in the family we had installed a fairly large water heater, but it wasn't big enough that day. I didn't want to answer the question, but the Lord made it clear I was not to get out of the shower without answering. So as time dragged on, I had to start turning the cold water down and the hot water up until I got to the magical moment when the cold water was completely off and the hot water was full hot, but the water coming out was now ice cold anyway.

At this point I turned the showerhead as far down and toward the wall as it would go. I stood back as far away as I could get and was now only getting a slight spray of cold water on me.

Even though I can be a very stubborn person, at times I realized that this was a no-win situation and decided if I didn't answer soon, my skin might permanently stay in the raisin-type condition it was now in.

I got down on my knees and began to pray earnestly. I asked the Lord how my dying could possibly advance the kingdom one bit, but to my surprise the Lord became totally silent. We had just been having great dialogue before, give and take, but now He was no longer talking. In my heart I knew why. He was not going to say anything else until I answered what He had asked me. He was waiting for me to do something with the last instruction He had given me.

Before I tell you what happened next, I think it would be worth mentioning that there are many Christians today who would say they haven't heard from God in a while. I fully believe this is sometimes because He is waiting for us to do something with the last thing He told us. Very often we could track our dry spell of not hearing Him right back to a certain event or situation where we chose to ignore Him. If that would describe you, then know this: God wants relationship with us, and when we run back to Him, He is waiting with open arms!

I finally decided to answer the question and was able to say with complete sincerity I would die for the advancement of the kingdom—on one condition: God would send my wife a husband who would love her more than I did and that this man would also love my children more than I did. I know we shouldn't try to make deals with God, but I've found that desperation tends to bring those tendencies up in us humans.

I loved my family so much that somewhere in my mind I thought this might be an impossible request for God, for Him to find someone who would love them more than me, but He immediately replied that it was a done deal. When I realized what I had just agreed to, I began to weep bitterly. The cold water spraying on me no longer seemed to matter.

When I got out of the shower, I walked to our closet and looked inside. My wife's clothes are on the right and my clothes are on the left. As I stood in the doorway, the thought came to me that someone else's clothes were going to be on the left side of the closet at some point. I looked around at the house we built and thought about another man getting to enjoy it. I turned around and looked at our bed and felt sick to my stomach as I thought of another man lying in it with my wife.

Just then I caught movement through the window, and I noticed my children playing outside. This was the final blow that made me begin to cry again as I envisioned another man getting to raise my children and enjoy their company as well. I waited a few days before calling Pastor Ryan and telling him I had answered the question from God. When I did, he said that quite possibly it was like the story in the Bible of Abraham getting asked to offer his only son Isaac. He believed it was a test and I had passed.

I then told Him about the deal I had made with God for Him to send a replacement for me who would love Lori and the kids more than I did. Pastor Ryan was the only person I had mentioned this whole situation to, so I asked him to call Lori and tell her about our conversation if and when anything happened to me. He laughed at me and said I must have heard wrong because that didn't sound like God to him, as God wouldn't plant fear in my heart.

The Final Warning

Fall had turned to winter. On Tuesday, November 14, 2006, I took the truck apart that would end up falling on me two days later. I had also finished up another small job that day. By the time I got home from work that night, it was late. Lori had already put the kids to bed, but she had saved me a plate of supper.

She heated it up in the microwave and put it in front of me as I sat down at the head of the table. The type of work I did was often very physical, and after putting in more than twelve hours that day, I was ready to just sit down and rest in silence as I ate my supper.

My wife on the other hand wanted some adult interaction after being alone with our four young children and began to try and talk to me, but I just sat there, not responding as she spoke.

After making small talk for a while, she brought up a subject that she and I had not talked about before, and although it shouldn't have, it took me completely by surprise. She said we needed to close our business immediately and put it up for sale. She began to get strangely agitated and begged me to not go back to work tomorrow. She continued by telling me that we were called into full-time ministry as a family and that we were being disobedient by not doing it. Her sense of urgency about the situation seemed very out of character and unreasonable to me.

At this point we began to have a strong disagreement. (For those of you who aren't married, that is code for "bad argument.")

I asked her who was going to pay our several thousand dollars of monthly bills if I just quit working. Did she have a hidden money tree out in the woods that I didn't know about? She then proceeded to tell me that I was a hypocrite because she had heard me tell several people over the last year at the Bible studies and home groups I led to have faith in God, but I didn't have faith in God for our finances.

I don't know about you, but the only thing that gets me really mad in an argument is the truth, so I blew up. I slammed my fist down on the table as hard as I could and told her to just leave me alone.

She stood up from her chair and pointed at me with her finger about an inch from the end of my nose and repeated three times, "What is it going to take for you to be obedient to God?" Two days later I found out exactly what it was going to take for me to be obedient.

The Accident

The day the accident happened started out just like any other day at work for me. I left my house early that morning in the cold and had driven my service truck that contained all my tools and equipment to the job site almost an hour away. I was there to fix a coolant leak on the engine of a Peterbilt logging truck. I had diagnosed the problem and disassembled the engine two days earlier on a Tuesday; it was now Thursday, November 16.

The replacement parts I needed to finish the job had arrived, and we spent all day reassembling the engine inside the nice warm garage. I was working with the part-time driver, part-time mechanic from the logging company who helped me on the entire job.

At the end of the day we started the engine to test the repair to make sure it was no longer going to leak coolant. The truck was not completely back together, but the technical items were done and the man I was working with would be able to finish up the truck the next day by himself.

As we waited for the engine to get warm, I began to wipe my tools off and put them away in my truck. In just a few minutes I would be driving home, and I was looking forward to getting there and eating supper. The man walked up behind me and tapped me on the shoulder. He asked if I would take a look at one more thing before I left. I glanced at the clock and saw that it was about 6:10 p.m.

He said that there was an oil seep on the engine that had been there for a long time, but he couldn't figure out where it was coming from. I asked what area it was in. He pointed to the front of the engine near the bottom.

This particular semitruck was a conventional or long nose, which means it had a hood and fenders. In the front of the truck was a large chrome bumper that was tall and went from one side to the other. If you were to look underneath that bumper toward the rear of the truck, you would see that the lowest thing to the ground is the front axle that goes between the two front wheels. It is called a dropped axle because after attaching to the wheels on each side, it immediately drops down and is close to the ground all the way from one side of the truck to the other.

There is about five to six tons of weight on this axle when the truck is not loaded. So these ten thousand to twelve thousand pounds of weight rest on just the two front wheels alone. The man I was working with had removed the passenger's side front wheel so we could get the engine hoist close enough to the engine to lift off the cylinder head and put it back on.

In order to remove the front wheel, he had placed a round bottle jack under the front axle and had jacked it up until the wheel was off of the ground and could be removed. Unfortunately there was no jack stands or blocking of any type under the axle at this point, and all that weight was resting on this small bottle jack.

To find the source of his oil seep I had to get under the truck, so I lay down on my back on his creeper and began to roll underneath the front bumper, feet first. Before going entirely under the truck I stopped and asked him to get up in the cab and see what the engine temperature was. I then continued to go under the truck until my head was under the front of the running engine, which put the axle that had been jacked up just above my stomach area.

When he climbed up in the cab, the truck shifted ever so slightly, and I caught movement in the peripheral vision of my left eye. I turned my head just in time to see the bottle jack wiggle and then fly out from underneath the axle like a rocket. The axle crashed to the cement with a tremendous bang and in doing so came down across my midsection like a blunt guillotine, crushing my body in half!

God Sends His Angels

Without thinking I grabbed the I-beam shaped axle and tried to bench press it off of my body. The ten-thousand- to twelve-thousand-pound mass didn't budge, and the grave reality of what just happened dropped into my head as fast as the axle had fallen on me. From the deepest part of my soul I called out twice, "Lord, help me!"

On impact blood had shot up my throat from the inside out and entered my mouth, so I turned my head and spit out the initial blob.

In fear I looked down at my stomach area where the axle had fallen on me and could only see about an inch of air space between the bottom of the axle and the cement on the left side of my body and about two inches of air space on the right side of my body. By this I knew that the left side of my body was around an inch thick and the right side was around two inches thick. I also knew the axle was about six inches wide or deep from the front to the back, so even though I couldn't see the lower half of my body, I knew I was flattened out from about the bottom of my ribs to the top of my pelvic bone and from one side to the other.

The driver got down out of the truck and called 911 before trying to get the truck off of me. He could no longer put the jack under the axle because the axle was now resting on the cement, so he placed the jack under the passenger's side leaf spring and began to jack it up from there. I begged him not to position the jack there because I was afraid the jack was going to slip out again due to the curve of the spring. He didn't have a choice and continued to jack it up despite my concerns.

Once he got the truck off of me, I looked down. I remember thinking that I looked like a cartoon character that had something heavy fall on it and it became paper thin. It was hard to believe what had just happened was real, but the incredible pain I felt proved it was.

I begged him to get me out from under the truck, but he could tell by how thin I was across the middle that my spine must be broken, so he refused to move me for fear he would hurt me even worse. I continued to plead with him to move me out from under the truck as I was afraid the jack was going to slip and it was going to fall on me again, but I soon realized he wasn't going to.

In desperation I grabbed the bottom of the large chrome bumper that was back behind my head and decided I would drag myself out from under the truck if it was the last thing I did. It took everything

I had to do it, but I was able to pull myself out enough that now my head was just sticking out from under the big chrome bumper, with the rest of my body still under the truck. I then lost all strength, my eyes closed, and everything faded away.

At that point my spirit left my body and went up into the ceiling of the garage. The Bible tells us that we have a spirit that lives inside our body, and when we die our spirit leaves our earthly shell. This is the reason why there are literally millions of people who have encountered these "out-of-body" experiences at the time of some trauma or other life-and-death situation.

As I looked down from above, it was as if I were just an observer to what was happening below. I was in a state of perfect peace with no pain and no sorrow. I could clearly see the head of a man sticking out from under the front bumper of the truck and could also see another man on his knees above him. The man on his knees was crying and running his fingers through the hair of the other man as he talked to him, but the other man's eyes were closed and he wasn't responding. I listened to every word the kneeling man said as he repeatedly apologized.

For some reason at this point I didn't know that the hurt man under the truck was me. I'm sure this was partly why I could feel perfect peace and had no sense of sorrow about the situation. I continued to watch from my vantage point in the ceiling, focused intently on the two men beneath me, when all of a sudden my view seemed to broaden out. I now saw that there were two huge angels, one on each side of the men below!

The angels were identical in appearance and were on their knees facing the front of the truck just as the man in the middle was, although their heads stuck up a couple of feet higher than his did. This would have made them about eight feet tall if they had been standing up. There was light emanating from both of them, and they were strikingly visible, with no fuzziness or cloudiness as is sometimes depicted in paintings or movies.

They did not have wings either but were wearing robes that were made out of a thick material I had never seen before. This strange material caught my attention, and I noticed that it appeared to be made up of small ropes woven together. The robes were tight enough that I could see that these two angels were very muscular. They each had their arms positioned under the front bumper, angled in toward the body of the man under the truck. Although I couldn't see their hands, it was obvious from the positioning of their arms that they must have been touching him.

They had long hair that went down their backs just to the level of the belts that were around their robes. From my view in the ceiling I couldn't see their faces, only their backs, but it was obvious they were men. They never moved or said a word, and they never acknowledged that I was in the ceiling above them either.

Decision Time

I continued to watch from above as the fire department personnel and emergency workers arrived at the scene of the accident. Eight of the ten people who arrived came in through the front or main entrance, while the last two people to get there came in through the back door. A year after the accident I spoke to the fire department that was called to the scene and was able to identify several of the people who came the night of the accident as well as point out the two people who had come in through the "wrong" door. I asked them why they had entered through the back door, and they were able to explain what had happened, causing them to come in through the back door. Although these are little details, they are important because they prove I had an "out-of-body" experience; otherwise I would have had no way of seeing these things from under the truck, eyes closed.

One of the two people who came in the back door was a woman with long red hair, who I later found out was a first responder named Shannon Cila. She walked up to the driver's side of the truck and positioned herself above the man who was hurt. After a bit she began to pat the man on the cheek and tell him to open his eyes, although at that point she felt he was probably already dead because she couldn't find a pulse, his skin was pale and ashen, and his lips were blue. The two large angels remained on each side of the body, seemingly oblivious to the commotion around them. I continued to watch from above as she asked what his name was. After being told, she began to say, "Bruce Van Natta, open your eyes," while lightly slapping him on the cheek again. She continued doing this, getting louder each time as desperation and urgency climaxed.

For some reason this really caught my attention up there in the ceiling, although I wasn't sure why. With no warning the next thing I knew, my spirit had shot back into my body, and in the blink of an eye I was now face-to-face with the woman.

The first sensation that hit me was incredible pain. I felt as if a truck had fallen on me! The next thought that came to my mind was, "Oh, no, I'm the guy under the truck!" Then it all came back to me, and I clearly remembered the truck falling on me. I also remembered being up in the ceiling and seeing the two angels. For some reason it hadn't seemed like that big of a deal while my spirit was up in the ceiling, but now it was. I looked on each side of my body where the angels had been, but I could no longer see them.

We learned later that I had five places where major arteries were severed. I should have bled to death in just a few minutes or about the time my spirit left my body. In fact, when my case is compared to the data from some major studies that were done on arteries being severed, doctors make the claim they can't find anybody else in the world who has lived with major arteries being severed in five places as mine were.

Although I could no longer see the angels anymore, this proves to me that they were still there and were continuing to do what God had sent them to do—and that is keep me alive.

The pain was almost unbearable. I found that when I would close my eyes, total relief would come, as my spirit would leave my body again. The thing that was different now was that when my spirit left my body, it was no longer just going up to the ceiling, but it was going in a tube very fast to a place far away. When this happened, Shannon would begin to call my name loudly again until I opened my eyes. Unfortunately when I would open my eyes and my spirit would return, so would the horrendous pain!

In my head it was as if there were two voices competing for my attention. One was loud and gruff and kept telling me to just shut my eyes and give up and die, as I was going to go to heaven anyway. The other was quieter and simply said that if I wanted to live, I was going to have to fight, and it was going to be a hard fight.

These two opposing thoughts or voices continued to volley back and forth in my head. As they did, I found my spirit going in and out of my body. The only deciding factor seemed to be if I chose to close my eyes or not.

All of a sudden Shannon got my attention when she told me that I needed to fight as I was on the verge of life or death! Her statement was so close to the quiet Whisper in my head that I knew it couldn't be a coincidence. I realized God was now speaking through her, saying the same thing again. I contemplated what was happening with my spirit and knew what she said was true. She then asked me if I had a wife or kids or anything else I could fight for.

From the moment that the truck had fallen on me, everything else had faded away. The thought of being married or even Lori and the kids had not crossed my mind until Shannon said what she did.

As soon as she asked what I had to fight for, I remembered my wife and four young children who needed a husband and a father. I decided right then and there that I would fight for them and keep my eyes open no matter how bad it hurt.

Because of the extremely rural location of the accident and some transportation issues, it took much time, but I was eventually med-flighted to one of the largest trauma centers in our state. The doctors were astounded at what they found. It had now been over two hours since the truck had fallen on me. The CT scans and other tests seemed to show I had severed arteries and veins, which had caused me to bleed out into my stomach cavity. By all accounts I should have bled to death in just a few minutes. This caused great confusion because my eyes were open and I was obviously still alive, although unable to verbally communicate. One of the doctors later commented that when he looked at the CT scan images that night, they looked like they were from a dead person, but my heart was pounding as if I was running a marathon.

I was immediately given massive blood transfusions, but instead of my blood pressure coming up, it remained critically low and then dropped to nothing, causing all kinds of alarms to go off. When this happened, everything began to grow dim for me, and although I hadn't been able to speak a single word up until this moment, I shocked and surprised the doctors by blurting out that if they didn't so something to help me right then, I was going to die! At that point I was rushed into emergency surgery. I fought to keep my eyes open right up until they put me out with the anesthesia.

During the initial surgery they made an incision from the bottom of my ribs to the top of my pelvic bone so they could completely open up the damaged area and inspect it. What they found looked like mush. The impact had completely severed, chopped, and pulverized my small intestine as well as everything else in that area of the abdomen.

The head of the trauma department had been called in from home. After seeing how extensive my injuries were, he made the decision that they would only reconnect the severed arteries and veins at that time after removing the badly injured ones. He came out and told my wife that in all his years as a trauma doctor he had never see anyone make it to the hospital alive with the injuries I had—and they didn't expect me to live through the night.

My wife and others from my family and church decided to praise God for every thirty minutes of life I was given. So they would gather in a circle, hold hands, and thank Him after every thirty minutes that I was alive. As the minutes turned to hours, morning arrived, and the doctors were surprised my heart was still beating.

They ended up operating on me again that next morning for several hours. My broken ribs, fractured vertebrae, and damaged pancreas, stomach, and spleen took a back seat while they worked to deal with more life-threatening problems. My crushed abdomen swelled up so badly that it was not able to be closed up for six more days. I was kept in an induced coma for weeks to help the healing process.

Sweet Bread Man Comes to Pray

The average adult has about 600 centimeters or 19.5 feet of small intestines. Most of mine were destroyed, and the doctors were only able to save two sections that equaled about 100 centimeters or 3.2 feet of total length. To make matters worse, the most important parts of the small intestine, the ileum as well as the duodenum, were basically gone, so I would need to rely on being fed intravenously in addition to the feeding tube to stay alive.

The night of the accident I weighed well over 180 pounds, but just three months later I was down to 125 pounds and people said I looked like someone from a concentration camp. I had gone through four surgeries by that point, and the last one had been to remove a portion of the small intestine they had tried to save. I was slowly starving to death. One day a doctor came in and told us they could only keep me alive for about another year to year and a half at the most with the IV feeding, as the small amount of intestine I had left wasn't able to absorb the needed nutrients.

My wife and others had my name put on prayer lists and prayer chains all over the country, including at my friend Pastor Ryan's church. After we were told I wasn't expected to live very long, the intensity of those prayers increased as day by day I continued to lose weight.

One morning the Lord woke up Bruce Carlson (the man the Lord had shown me in the sweet bread dream before I met him on vacation) and told him to fly to Wisconsin and pray over me. When he told his wife what he thought he heard, they ended up deciding that it must have just been an emotional thought and not God as there were people we went to church with who could and would pray for me.

The next morning at the same time he was awoken again, and the Lord again put on his heart that he was to buy a plane ticket and fly to Wisconsin to pray for me, and if he did, God was going to do a miracle. This time he was obedient and ended up buying the ticket and flying from New York to pray for me.

Some friends from my church picked him up at the airport and brought him to the hospital. They sang a few songs in the room, and then Bruce Carlson prayed. He started by asking the Lord to heal me and then said that he was adding his prayers to all the other prayers that had gone up for me around the country already.

At that point he placed his right palm on my forehead and began to pray in a way that was much different than anyone else had prayed for me. He spoke to the "mountain" as Jesus taught us to, and he used the "authority" that has been granted to all believers. My "mountain" was a physical problem caused from the lack of intestines, so he simply said with power, "Small intestine, I command you to supernaturally grow in length right now in the name of Jesus!"

When he said that, it felt like electricity had come out of his hand and into my body. It was like I had touched an electric fence and had gotten shocked. But instead of staying at the point of contact, the electricity traveled right down into my belly. Immediately I began to feel something cylindrical moving around inside of my stomach.

I turned to Brian Strong, my friend who had brought Bruce Carlson to the hospital, and told him it felt like a snake had just come uncoiled inside my stomach, as it was the only way I could verbalize what I was feeling.

My weight immediately leveled off, and before long I began to gain weight, which puzzled the doctors. Several tests were done, and we found out God had truly done another amazing miracle—and not just a healing miracle but a creative miracle! CT scans, X-rays, and an upper GI all concluded I had miraculously gained 6 to 8 feet or at least 200 centimeters of small intestine from nowhere! It is the reason I am alive six years later and am able to live a normal life and now have a normal length of life expectancy.

God Is Looking for Warriors

I personally think one of the most interesting things about my accident experience is that the Lord gave *me* the choice if I wanted to live or die. Clearly it was the enemy who told me to just give up and die, because he always promotes death. The Holy Spirit said *if I wanted to live, then I was going to have to fight.* God is a God of free will, and He always has been, going all the way back to the Garden of Eden. He could have easily stopped Adam and Eve from eating the fruit, but because He had given them free will, He allowed them to make their own choice.

In the same way He still gives people freewill choices today. We get to choose if we are going to believe in Him or not as our Lord and Savior. We get to choose if we are going to believe all the promises in the Bible or just some of them. We get to choose if we are going to be warriors and fight the fight of faith or not.

The night of the accident He not only gave me the choice to live or not, but He also warned me if I wanted to live, I was going to have to fight and it was going to be a hard fight! God never lies to us as some well-meaning evangelist might. When we become Christians, it doesn't mean our lives are now going to be easy. In fact, many times just the opposite happens, and it gets harder in some ways. The good news is that no matter what happens, God will never leave us or forsake us. He will always empower us to be victorious in our battles if we go to Him. Jesus said in John 16:33, "In this world you will have trouble. But take heart! I have overcome the world."

That night I didn't know I would end up having five major surgeries and get stuck in the hospital on and off for over a year. I also didn't know there would be a long period of time after that where I would be very sick and weak, but He did. God also knew there would be a few days in the hospital that I would be so sick and in so much pain I would ask Him to just let me die if I wasn't going to get better.

God knew all these things, and that is why He warned me I would have to fight and that it would be a hard fight. Maybe as you're reading this you are going through some battles in your own life. If you are, then know this: God is looking for warriors who will fight the good fight of faith. If we choose to take the challenge, we will be on the winning team. Period! But if we decide not to fight, how can we ever expect to be victorious?

When David showed up in the Valley of Elah the day he fought Goliath, the whole Israelite army had already been there forty days, and not one man had come forward to fight the giant. All God needed was one person who would have faith in Him to do what He had promised to do. When the little shepherd boy came forward with that faith, God used him to defeat the giant.

Some days the giant you're facing might seem too big, too mean, or too strong, but that is when we have to know the God we serve is bigger and stronger than any enemy we could ever face.

Or maybe the problem might be we don't feel like a warrior. Sometimes we feel more timid than bold or softer than strong. If that is the case, then receive the message found in 1 John 4:4. It says that the One who is in you is greater/stronger than the one who is in the world.

That's right. God lives in you, a believer, and there isn't anybody He is afraid of. There isn't anybody who is greater or stronger than He is either. He just asks that we would believe in Him and His promises. The King of kings is on our side and is taking up residence in us, so even if we don't feel like a warrior, it doesn't matter because the greatest One lives inside of us.

Knowing this will affect not only your future but also the future of those God has placed in your life. I have often wondered what would have happened to me if Bruce Carlson had not chosen to say yes when God asked him to be a giant slayer and fly to Wisconsin and pray for me. It would not be an exaggeration to say that if the Lord had not sent someone else, I would have just wasted away until I died. We are dependent upon each other in the body of Christ, and our personal decisions not only affect ourselves, but they also often affect others more than we realize.

God is looking for warriors, and the only qualification they need is to believe that He is faithful. Yes, there will be a fight, but when you enlist with the King of kings, victory is attainable every time!

Chapter 4

The Winds of Pentecost in Our Bedroom

IN THE YEAR following the accident I spent a lot of time in the hospital, but because my insurance wasn't that good, I was sent home sometimes in between operations for weeks to months. Nurses were assigned to care for me at home and would regularly come in to help with the IVs and other things my wife couldn't do.

My attitude and temperament began to deteriorate as the seemingly endless cycle of sickness-operation-recovery dragged on. I believe this was for three main reasons. For one, my personality type is extremely active, and to be stuck in the hospital or even my own bed for that matter unable to "do" things was very hard on me.

The second factor was that because my injuries were so severe and extensive, I was constantly in a lot of pain. It was really hard to stay positive when I was so weak and sick and had to deal with the never-ending pain. Doctors had me on the absolute strongest pain medications available, and I think this was the cause of the third reason why my attitude had gotten so bad.

I no longer could hear God's voice at all. Before the accident I was having detailed conversations with God daily, but afterward it was if He had moved away.

Now don't get me wrong. I knew that He loved me and had sent the angels to save me. In fact, the very first thing I tried to communicate to my wife after they took me out of the induced coma was that I had seen two huge angels. It had been so profound I wanted to tell everybody—doctors, nurses...anybody who would listen, but my fear of what they might think held me back at times.

The Real Question

In between my fourth and fifth major operations I was asked if I would share my testimony at that little country church of my grandpa and grandma's I told you about in chapter 1. It was the first place I had heard about Jesus and His love as a child some thirty-two years earlier, so I guess it was fitting the Lord sent me there to be the first place to officially share my testimony, although I have to admit I was very scared to stand up in front of the people and talk.

One day not long after speaking at the little country church, I was sitting at our kitchen table reading my Bible and praying. When I read the Bible before the accident, the words were powerful and alive to me. Since the accident they had somehow become just words. Before, my prayers had been intimate conversations with God. But after, they too had become just words. There was no longer any life in them either. Looking back on it now, I believe that the heavy medications I was taking were the cause for this, but at the time I didn't understand what was happening.

Even though I had seen the angels God sent and knew He had done a huge miracle by saving my life, I was miserable inside because I missed the daily relationship and interaction we used to have. I couldn't take it anymore and ended up throwing a fit.

I slammed the Bible shut and loudly called out to God question after question. "Where are You? Why don't You talk to me anymore? Why did You even bother to save me if we can't be close now? When am I ever going to get better?" I continued having my pity party until there was nothing left for me to say.

Sitting there in the silence I heard God speak to me for the first time in several months. Interestingly enough He ignored every question I had just asked Him during my tantrum and instead asked me a question. He asked if I remembered our conversation in the shower when I had told Him I would die for the advancement of His kingdom. He then reminded me of my one condition—that He send a replacement who would love Lori and the kids more than I did. I told him I did remember. Then He told me He had kept His end of the deal.

This didn't make any sense to me as I was still alive. He again told me that He had kept His end of the deal. I finally asked Him to please explain it to me. He said that it was me. I was the replacement husband and father who now loved my wife and kids more than I used to. It was true. The accident had caused my priorities to change and had opened my eyes to what was really important in life. My family was a big part of that. Even though I loved them a lot before, I loved and appreciated them now more than I used to. I began to cry as I realized His mercy and grace in the situation I hadn't understood before.

He went on to say I had been misrepresenting Him when I told people the accident story and how He had asked me if I would die for the advancement of the kingdom. I said, "But Lord, You did ask me if I would die for the advancement of the kingdom, and when I said yes, then the accident happened."

The Lord explained that although these were true statements, I had completely misunderstood His question. Each time He had asked if I would die for the advancement of the kingdom, He wasn't talking about a one-time physical death but a death to self every day! He was asking if I would lay down my plans, agendas, and desires in order to do His will. (This is something He is asking all Christians to do, including you.)

From the day He had called my name in that church there had been a call on my life for full-time ministry, but I had never accepted it. Over and over throughout the years He had confirmed it through so many different avenues, but I had always gone my own way instead. Months before the accident the Lord told Pastor

Ryan I was to be an evangelist. I asked God to tell me Himself; He did, but I still didn't listen.

The Lord then reminded me He had sent my wife two days before the accident to try and change my mind, but again I had refused His call. That night under the leading of the Holy Spirit she had begged me not go back to work as a mechanic again, but that we sell the business and go into ministry as a family.

I began to think a lot about the accident and what caused it. In John 10:10 Jesus taught us that the devil comes to steal, kill, and destroy, but that He came that we might have life and have it to the full or abundantly. God wants the best for us, but He gives us free will, and when we don't make the right choices, we sometimes have to suffer consequences. I believe the accident happened because my continued disobedience in this area had made me vulnerable to an attack from the devil. God knew what the enemy was planning and He kept trying to get me to change direction to prevent it, but I hadn't listened.

Accepting the Call

After everything that happened, it was now obvious even to someone as simple and stubborn as me that I had no choice but to be in full-time ministry. I decided I would go back to the church the Lord had called my name in nearly twenty years earlier so I could repent and then accept His call instead of running away this time. I knew I didn't have to do it this way, but it somehow seemed right.

I made the two-hour drive to the church and went inside. It was empty because it was in the middle of the week, so I was able to move around until I found the exact spot I had been sitting when God called my name. Even though almost twenty years had passed, the memory of it was still very vivid. I bowed my head and began to pray. I asked the Lord to forgive me for being so hardheaded and disobedient and for running away from His call all this time.

As I prayed, I started to get a sorrow deep in my heart for all the years I had wasted. It wasn't condemnation or guilt but godly sorrow for not doing what I had been called to do. There was the realization that my choice had affected not just me but also many others. I could really feel a strong presence of God's glory in the place now, and all of a sudden the Holy Spirit told me to lift my head up and open my eyes.

When I did, the Lord opened my spiritual eyes and I could see there were several white-robed angels sitting in all the seats around me. Each one of them had their heads bowed too, and there was a very solemn yet powerfully reverential feeling to it all. It made me understand even more what a serious thing this was and that my previous disobedience as well as current choice to accept this call wasn't to be taken lightly.

The Lord reminded me of the prophetic words spoken over me a few months before the accident by Pastor Ralph Diaz in New York. He had said I would be seeing angels soon. Although it wasn't how I had imagined it, I did get to see them the night of the accident and again seated around me in the church. He had also said that I would go into full-time ministry and the glory of the Lord would surround the ministry and me. This too was being fulfilled as I answered God's call in the church that day. The weightiness of His presence seemed to hem me in.

Sweet Bread Revealed

In fact, every single thing Pastor Diaz spoke over me came true, including my meeting someone very important to my future while I was on that vacation. It obviously had been Bruce Carlson, the man God showed me in the sweet bread dream. He was the one God had chosen to send to pray for my intestines to grow back. His obedience was the reason I had not starved to death.

When I asked the Lord what I should name the ministry I was to start, He immediately told me Sweet Bread Ministries. I was obedient to do it, but I have to admit I was somewhat uncomfortable with the name at first—that was until I spoke at a certain church and the pastor gave me insight into what it really meant. After sharing my testimony, he asked me why I had chosen the name Sweet Bread Ministries. I explained the dream about eating sweat bread with the man who ended up coming to pray for me and how the miracle had then happened.

He got very emotional and began to say how profound that was. I believed he was referring to the fact that the Lord had shown me Bruce Carlson in the dream before I met him and how he ended up coming to pray for me. But he said that was only part of it. He asked me if I knew what the term "sweet bread" meant. I replied that to me it was sweet-tasting bread with frosting on it.

He was shocked I didn't know its other meaning and told me the term *sweetbread* describes something entirely different in other parts of the world. He walked over to his computer and typed "sweetbread" into a search engine and then printed off one of the descriptions he found. It said sweetbread was the cooked pancreas, stomach, and intestines from a lamb or calf! All of these things had been badly damaged in my accident. My intestines were what were healed, and several feet of them had grown back when Bruce Carlson had come to pray for me!

The sweet bread dream that the Lord had given me now took on much more significance as we realized the symbolic meaning of what the sweet bread really stood for. In the dream God had not only shown me Bruce Carlson weeks before I met him, which was incredible enough, but also then symbolically showed that he would come to me and we would then get to share this "sweetbread" or intestinal miracle.

Battles With Fear

There was another part of the dream that was also important. At the end of the dream I had become fearful that I would have to share the sweet bread with others. The Lord told me because it was a gift I should share and be happy about it.

After the accident and accepting the call into full-time ministry, it became clear to me the reason I didn't want to share was because of fear. Fear had caused me not to tell anyone about Jesus hugging me as child for over twenty years and had prevented me from sharing the reality of God with other people when I had been given the chance before also.

The fear was for many reasons. I was afraid people might not believe me. I was afraid people would think I was crazy or weird. I was afraid people would look at who I was and all the mistakes I had made and say that I was a hypocrite and had no right to tell anyone else about God. I was afraid to fail and look foolish. I was also afraid to have anybody ask me questions I didn't know the answers to because I believed my knowledge of God was inadequate.

The Lord started to show me that these fears that kept me from going into ministry in the first place could all be boiled down to one thing: fear of man. Over time the Lord began to remove these fears from me as He taught me to look to Him alone for my approval and success, but it was a process.

I was still not fully physically recovered when I said yes to God's call on my life for full-time ministry. Still He began to send me small opportunities to share my testimony. Each time I would be consumed with fear for days before the event. When it came time to stand in front of the people, all those fears would come crashing down on me, causing me to sweat and tremble. As I spoke, I would have a hard time staying focused as my mind would listen to these fearful thoughts and become intimidated.

This put me in a dilemma as I had told the Lord I would go into ministry, but when the chance arose, I would still sometimes resist out of fear. I wanted to share the "sweet bread," the testimony of the miracles God had done for me, but it frightened me greatly.

God began to give me dreams that showed me what was going on and what was at stake. In one dream a faceless man was standing in front of me holding a running chainsaw. The tip or nose of the chainsaw bar was in my mouth, and I was biting down as hard as I could on the bar while holding my lips and cheeks back so that I wouldn't get cut by the rotating chain. Although he never spoke, I knew the faceless man wanted me to open my mouth, but I was afraid to, so I wouldn't. All of a sudden he moved the saw from side to side, cutting my cheeks back to the jaw joint, and I opened my mouth expecting to feel pain or see blood, but there was none. I felt my cheeks with my hands and realized that not only was I unhurt, but also that my mouth was now wide open and it felt good.

As I mentioned before, in my dreams a faceless man always represents the Holy Spirit, and God was symbolically showing me He wanted me to open my mouth. He was also showing me that He would help me to do it and that even though I was afraid, it wouldn't hurt.

The very next night I had a dream as if I were watching from outer space. I saw a man who was supernaturally running from continent to continent around the earth looking for someone to help him, but he couldn't find help anywhere. As he ran, the surface of the earth kept getting hotter and hotter. He was trying to get away from the heat, but there was nowhere to go. He began to cry out in pain as fire started to shoot out from cracks in the ground. It was hard to watch, and I felt bad for the man as I knew he was going to die. All of a sudden the Lord asked if I would go to help him. This was clearly a dream where the Lord was asking me to help others find their way to eternal salvation. Again the Lord was asking me to open my mouth for the benefit of other people.

Not long after this I prayed to God asking Him to empower me and fill me with the Holy Spirit so that I would be able to accomplish what He wanted. I then had a dream where a hurricane force wind blew on me so hard I was barely able to stand and began to get blown backward. I soon found out this was a prophetic sign of what was about to happen.

Pentecost in Our Bedroom

I began to pray steadily that the Lord would remove these fears from me so I could do what He had called me to do. When I was talking with someone one-on-one, the fears never seemed to bother me, but when I had to speak in front of a group, that is when I became intimidated. At this point I had only spoken a handful of times and only to small groups and small churches, but some people from my church began to put a community event together where I was to be the speaker and there would potentially be hundreds of people attending.

The event was scheduled for Sunday night, October 28, 2007, which was about a year after my accident. As the event grew closer and closer, my fears continued to rise. Each time I heard a radio ad for the service or saw a poster advertising it, my blood ran cold.

The Friday night before the event I was asked to minister to a man who had just gotten out of prison. I was happy to do it to help take my mind off of the upcoming service. He was a lifelong drug and alcohol user, as I had been, and we had some other things in common, so we could relate to each other quite well. He was going through some hard times and needed help and he knew it, so by the end of the night he had chosen to accept Jesus as his Lord and Savior.

After leading him through a prayer to ask God into his heart, I began to try and explain to him what he could expect in the Christian life and how great God was. He was concerned that the good feeling he now had would go away as soon as I left or the next day. Because we both had used drugs for so long, I decided to try and use an analogy from that lifestyle he would understand. I told him the Holy Spirit was more powerful than any kind of drug or alcohol he could imagine. I went on to say he didn't have to worry about it wearing off because God had now come to live inside of him and he could get into God's presence any time he chose—and there were no negative side effects!

I spent almost the whole next day in prayer because of my fear of having to speak on Sunday in front of hundreds of people. I was afraid people who knew me would call me a hypocrite for talking about God or somebody would show up and call me out in front of the crowd for my past sins or illegal activities. Most of all I was afraid of standing up there and making a fool of myself because of not knowing what to say or how to say it. I knew the Holy Spirit was going to have to show up, or I was in big trouble. Without His guidance and power I would fail miserably.

That night I only slept for ten to twenty minutes at a time before I would wake up and desperately call out to God. Unfortunately I kept waking up Lori with my loud prayers. When she would awaken, I would ask her to pray for me also. Over and over throughout the night I begged God to send the Holy Spirit to me in great measure so that this first big service of the ministry wouldn't be a failure.

At about 3:30 a.m. the Lord gave me a dream that Lori and I were in a hospital waiting room. It seemed like we had been waiting forever to see the doctor when a nurse came into the room and led us down a hall that had many doors in it. She told us to go into the exam room that had the red light on above the door, and the doctor would come in and see us.

When we went into the room, we found that the outer wall of the exam room adjoined a bar or common drinking saloon. There was a window in the wall, and we could see right into the bar and watched as people were partying and drinking. I mentioned to Lori that I thought it was poor taste for the hospital to keep the window there and that they should block it off as it was a little offensive to have a window looking into a bar in an exam room. We had both quit drinking at this point in our lives, and I didn't want to have to think about that lifestyle because it had caused so many problems in the past for both of us.

At that time the nurse walked back in carrying what looked like a round bar tray that had two full shot glasses on it. She said the doctor had ordered our medicine and here it was. I argued with her that the doctor had never even come into the room and seen us, but she said I was wrong. He had been there, and this was the medicine he ordered. I tried to argue with her some more, but she handed us the shot glasses and told us very forcefully to just drink the medicine.

Lori and I clanked the shot glasses together as you would in a bar and then tilted our heads back and guzzled the medicine down. At that exact second I was awakened from the dream by the sound of a gale force wind in our bedroom. I was lying on my back in our bed, and the wind was causing the sheet to flap against the left side of my face. The heavy curtains on our windows were blown out at about a forty-five-degree angle, which allowed the bright light from a full moon to illuminate our otherwise dark bedroom. The wind seemed to be going in a circle in our room like a cyclone.

It was overwhelming to me, and I yelled out, "Heeeeeelp!" like a scared little girl. I heard Lori say something but couldn't make it out because the sound of the wind was too loud. After a few long moments the wind died down, and our room became dark again as the curtains came back into place and blocked out the moonlight once more.

I asked Lori, "Did you hear that?" She said she had heard me scream but couldn't move or open her eyes because incredible power was coming out of my hand and going into her face and head right then. Lori had been sleeping facedown in her pillow, and my right hand was underneath her pillow, palm up, directly under her face when the wind started up. She said at the time it was like an electric kaleidoscope. Colors with power had come out of my hand, and it felt "intoxicating" and had completely overwhelmed her. Although she had never done hard drugs, she said she imagined the experience to be stronger than any illegal drug could ever be. When I had yelled out, "Help!" she cried out "I command this to stop in the name of Jesus!" and then felt led to add, "Unless it is the Holy Spirit."

I immediately realized that every bit of fear was now gone, and in its place were peace and joy. I also now had a great expectation of what the Lord was going to do at the service that day. Even though I had barely slept all night and it was still very early in the morning, I knew I couldn't go back to sleep as great excitement began to stir inside of me. This encounter caused me to do a complete turnaround from being fearful to feeling unstoppable. God had poured out the Holy Spirit on me, and the proof was in the changed outlook and mind-set.

Just in case anybody reading this is wondering, let me say that there were no open windows in our room that night, and our door was also closed. Not that it could cause it, but the furnace was not on either. So there was absolutely no earthly explanation for the strong wind that came in our room.

After this experience happened, I reread the account of Pentecost in Acts 2 and noticed for the first time that it says the "sound" of a great wind entered the house they were in when the Holy Spirit came. I can say that if the wind in our bedroom had been as strong as it "sounded" to me, our house would have easily been blown down. I also realized that when the Holy Spirit came upon the believers in the Upper Room, it had the same effect on them as it did on me: their fears were now gone, as evidenced by them leaving their locked room and going out to preach immediately.

God's Plan

The meeting ended up going well that day, and we saw the Lord do some amazing things in people's lives. Even though there were over three hundred people who attended, I was able to speak for almost two hours and never once was intimidated or scared.

God has a sense of humor. I find it thought provoking that He used the very words I had spoken to someone else the night before and then turned them around and used them on me through the dream. He even used what came out of Lori's mouth. She had no idea what I had said the previous night when she declared that what she felt was stronger than any illegal drug could ever be. Nor could she have known what I was dreaming when she said that the power was intoxicating. It was clear who the "Doctor" was in my dream, and that He had been in our room even though I hadn't discerned it. It was also apparent that He knew just what "medicine" I needed to help me and that He had sent it. He also brought me to realize it was poor taste to even begin to compare His power to something as lowly as drugs and alcohol.

I had told the ex-prisoner that once we ask God into our hearts, the Holy Spirit comes to live in us and we can get into His presence any time we choose. However, my own fears showed me I wasn't always believing this or living it myself.

God had not caused the fears that were inside of me. They were an emotional attack from the enemy, but when I earnestly prayed to the Lord, He used the situation to release His power in my life. When He did, I ended up in a place or condition far better off than I had been even before the fears.

In the same way it was not God's perfect will for my accident to happen, but because He is such an amazing God, He is able to make good come from bad. That's why Romans 8:28 can say, "And we know that in all things God works for the good of those who love Him, who have been called according to his purpose." Due to all the miracles that happened surrounding my accident, millions of people have now gotten to hear how real He is and how much He loves us even when we are not doing what we are supposed to.

Chapter 5

Commissioned by Jesus

AFTER ACCEPTING GOD's call on my life in the year following the accident, we shut our diesel repair business down. I wasn't physically able to do my job at that point, and instead of hiring someone to run it, we felt led by God that we were to end it. With no money coming in and no worker compensation insurance from the accident, we went through our savings in about a year, which is around the time I got out of the hospital from my last major operation. Our church held a benefit for our family that raised a good chunk of money, but because we had so many medical bills in addition to our normal monthly bills, we used that up also.

At that time I cashed out my retirement plan so that we had money to live on and wouldn't lose our house. It hurt to forfeit some of it due to the costly early withdrawal penalty, but we had no choice. It would be enough for us to live on for another eight or nine months while I went to rehabilitation therapy and continued to recover. We kept out what we would need for the next ninety days and put the rest in a ninety-day CD. The hospital ended up putting us on a monthly payment plan for the huge amount we owed them, which helped, but at that time it looked as though we would have to make payments to them for the rest of our lives.

The Lord had told us to start a ministry and had even given us the name (Sweet Bread Ministries), but we hadn't officially started the process of creating a 501(c)(3) nonprofit organization yet because of lack of funds. About that time my first book, *Saved by Angels*, was being published, and I was under contract to purchase the first three thousand copies, which was going to cost us between fifteen thousand and twenty thousand dollars also.

Other than the house we lived in, we only had two other possessions we could sell to get the money we needed to pay for the books and to start the nonprofit ministry. One was a piece of commercial land we owned that had already been for sale for a few years, and at the time there was nobody interested in buying it.

The other possession was an antique motorcycle I had owned for about twenty years. It was an all-original 1937 Harley Davidson dresser that was rare because it was one of only about fifteen hundred produced and had all the options available for that time period. It had taken me over fifteen years to get it the way I wanted it, and I had won some very prestigious national awards with it once it was finished. That motorcycle was not only my prized possession; it was also my connection to the hobby of antique motorcycles, which was a passion for me.

I have to admit that at different times during my life I had gone past just being passionate about the motorcycle and had become obsessed with it. For example, the first few years of our marriage I kept the motorcycle in our living room year-round even though I had a huge garage, which didn't make my wife very happy. I selfishly told her that I had owned the motorcycle for years before I met her and we came as a package deal. I also literally traveled around the country quite often looking for parts to make it better. I ended up investing hundreds of hours into it and spending thousands of dollars on it throughout the years, and the last thing I ever wanted to do was get rid of it.

Now the Lord began to let me know He wanted me to sell the motorcycle so we could pay for the books and start the ministry. Since the accident had happened, the bike had not been as important to me, but selling it was still a very hard thing to do. I advertised it and was able to sell it quickly as people from around the world made offers.

We used the money to pay all the state, federal, and legal fees to start the 501(c)(3) nonprofit organization and to have a professional website created for the ministry. We were also able to purchase a newer car to be used for ministry travel and to pay for the contracted *Saved by Angels* books, which Lori and I then donated directly to the ministry. We then bought all of the office equipment and other supplies that were needed for the ministry and used the little that was left over for a few more months of living expenses.

The bike became the seed that allowed us to start the ministry officially on January 1, 2008. I had just had my last major operation not long before this, and although I was in no shape to minister right then, we would be a certified and formal ministry at 12:01 a.m. on the first day of the new year.

Cloud of Witnesses

I decided to fast and pray on New Year's Eve and ended up going to bed around 10:00 p.m. A few hours into the new year and our official ministry start date something incredible happened. At around 2:00 to 3:00 a.m. the Lord gave me three very detailed dreams in a row that were about the end times. I awoke and lay on my stomach pondering them; then I got the overwhelming feeling that someone was watching me.

The room was pitch-black, so I couldn't see Lori, but I could hear her breathing heavy so I knew she was sound asleep and not looking at me. I rolled over onto my back, and that is when I saw it. There was what looked like a large round hole in our ceiling that went all the way to heaven. I could see an amazing blue sky and huge clouds at the top, and around the perimeter of the hole hundreds of people were looking over the edge and watching me. They were far enough away I couldn't see them perfectly clear, but I could tell they were of different skin colors and ages. I could also see they were dressed in different types of clothes representing people from different eras in history as well as different countries.

They weren't talking or trying to communicate but were intently staring down this hole at me. It made me very uncomfortable. I closed my eyes to try and make it go away, but I could still feel them staring. I opened my eyes again and realized there were even more people than I had originally noticed. It was quite overwhelming. I closed my eyes again and asked the Lord to make it stop, at which point it instantly did.

I began to pray and ask God what was the meaning of the vision. The Holy Spirit immediately told me to go read Hebrews 11 and 12. Chapter 11 is known as the faith chapter as it explains what faith is all about and how it looked in different people's lives throughout history. Chapter 12 then starts with this verse, "Therefore, since we are surrounded by such a great *cloud of witnesses*, let us throw off everything that hinders and the sin that so easily entangles, and let us run with perseverance the race marked out for us" (emphasis added).

I was only a few hours into the first official day of our new ministry, and the Lord was letting me know I would need faith and perseverance to run the race He had marked out for me. He was also letting me know that many others, "a great cloud of witnesses," had gone before me and had successfully overcome their own trials throughout the ages.

This wasn't the first time the Lord had talked to me about my faith or lack of it. He had brought it up several different ways, including in some dreams, one that I will share with you later where He showed me that my shield of faith (Eph. 6:16) was so thin it was almost transparent. (OUCH!)

God Cultivates Faith for Finances

As my wife had pointed out two days before the accident, one of the main reasons I had not gone into full-time ministry was because of my lack of faith about finances. It took over three years of being in ministry before the Lord ended up completely removing that from me, but He already started the process while I was recovering from the accident.

With no money coming in and having to use up our savings and cash out what little we had in our retirement plan, the financial security I felt before was evaporating fast. I had always thought of my Harley as a monetary safety net, as I knew it was worth a lot and if I ever got desperate for money I could always sell it. Now that I had sold it to start the ministry, that safety net was gone also. Our economic outlook was as grim as it had ever been considering the large amounts of money we owed and the fact that none was coming in.

The only asset we now had left in the world was a piece of land we owned in Janesville, Wisconsin, that had all of the equity from our first home tied up in it. It had already been for sale for two years at this point, and no serious buyers had come forward.

About then we got a letter in the mail from a ministry we had donated to in the past saying that for around twelve thousand dollars they could build a church in India that would accommodate three hundred people and drill a well that would help the whole village. As I read the letter I believed the Lord told me we were to send them the money to do this, but it seemed crazy to me considering our current economic condition. When Lori got home, I asked her to read the letter but didn't tell her what I thought the Lord had spoken. After she read it, she turned to me and said she felt we were supposed to send the money!

I grabbed her hands and we knelt on the floor to pray. I said, "Lord, if You want us to do this, then You need to sell our land in Janesville, and just so I can be sure it's You, send us a buyer within the next seven days." I stood up and wrote in my journal what we prayed and then told Lori if a buyer popped up in the next week after not having one in two years, it would have to be God.

Exactly seven days later my phone rang and a man asked if I still had the land for sale in Janesville! He said he was interested in buying it as soon as possible and would even pay what we wanted. We set up a tentative closing date that was about forty-five days away and began the legal process so that it could happen.

Once again I got down on my knees and began to pray. I thanked the Lord for sending a buyer and for doing it within the seven days so that I knew for sure it was His will for us to pay to have the church built and the well dug. I told God that as soon as we sold the land and I had the money in my hand, I would send out the check for twelve thousand dollars for the church and well.

Immediately the Holy Spirit told me that we weren't to wait, but that I was to use money from our ninety-day CD that was about to come due in two weeks. This was all the money we had in the world to live on, and God was asking me to give a big part of it away! This made no sense to me at all. It wasn't like we hadn't already tithed and even given far more than a tithe on this money before now, and besides, we didn't have any money coming in. What if the sale of the land fell through?

Two weeks later when the CD matured I went to the bank and removed what we needed to pay our expenses for the next three months and put the remainder in another ninety-day CD. I felt it was too much to ask for us to have to send twelve thousand dollars from the small amount we had left to live on, and the people in India would just have to wait a few more weeks for the money they needed until we sold the land.

Within a few days I got a call saying that the buyer's financing had fallen through. Part of me was relieved that we hadn't sent the money to India, and another part of me was troubled I hadn't been completely obedient. I had justified my actions to myself by thinking that I would do what God had asked me to do, just as soon as the land sold. Besides, what would a few extra weeks matter?

A month later we heard that a large manufacturing plant, the biggest employer in the region, was closing down in Janesville where we owned the land. Soon after that happened, many supporting industries and other businesses began to close in the area as the local economy crumbled within a short period of time.

About five months later the prospective buyer called and said that he was still trying to get financing elsewhere, but they would need a current appraisal of the land to move forward. After the appraisal was completed, we found out the value of our land had dropped over twenty thousand dollars because it was a commercial piece of property and commercial land values had dropped excessively due to all the businesses closing in that area. The man called back and said we should just relist the land with a Realtor as he was not able to get financing for the project now and was no longer interested.

Needless to say, I was extremely disappointed our land was now worth twenty thousand dollars less and the prospective buyer no longer wanted it. A few days later while in prayer the Lord told me if I would have trusted Him and sent the twelve thousand dollars when He told me to, the land deal would have gone through then. But because I hadn't, it now cost me an extra twenty thousand dollars. It was a twenty-thousand-dollar lesson, and because He knew how important money was to me, He knew it bothered me greatly, so He hoped I had learned from it.

He went on to say that He wanted me to go to the bank and cash out our current CD and send the twelve thousand for the church and well right now, as He had told me to do before. He then reminded me that this was a test and what had happened the last time I failed to do what He asked.

This time was even harder for many reasons. Our CD was not due at this moment, and if I cashed it out, I knew there would be a financial penalty. Even more importantly the twelve thousand was now half of what we had left to live on, and we currently didn't have a closing date to sell the land or even a buyer who was interested or could get financing!

I wrestled with the decision for eleven days before I went to the bank and cashed out the CD and sent off the check for twelve thousand dollars. The very next day the prospective buyer who had told us he was no longer interested called and said he had changed his mind and had found a way to pay for the land—and wanted it as soon as possible! Interestingly enough we ended up closing on the land eleven months after we had received the letter asking for the twelve thousand dollars.

We deposited the check into our checking account and decided after it cleared we would use most of it to put toward our current home loan as we had always planned and would use what we didn't apply to the home loan for living expenses.

A Bigger Test

Once the money became available in our account, I told my wife to write out a check for the majority of it to be applied to our home loan. Immediately the Holy Spirit told me not to do it, so I told Lori to just wait. Days turned to weeks and weeks turned to months, but we still didn't feel released by God to pay down our home mortgage for some unknown reason to us.

Then one day the Holy Spirit told me I was about to be tested again in the area of finances, but the stakes would be much higher this time. Within a short time the Lord put on both Lori's and my heart that we were to pay for the building of an orphanage in a third world country. When we prayed about how much to give, we were both given the same amount, which was about 60 percent of the total we had gotten for the land. We asked the Lord to now give us the details, as we didn't know where it was to be built or whom we were to work with. At this point we hadn't told a single soul what we felt the Lord was prompting us to do.

A few weeks later a friend invited us to their church to hear a traveling evangelist speak. That night the man mentioned that his ministry cared for orphans in Honduras, but the location they were in was dangerous and the community didn't want them there. He went on to say they also owned some vacant land out in the country and hoped to build a new orphanage there but didn't have the money to do it.

After the service Lori and I asked the man if he could find out how much it would cost to build the orphanage on his land in the country. He said they had previously drawn up the plans and gotten some estimates and knew an approximate price already. When he told us the cost, it was the exact amount the Lord had already told us we were to give to build an orphanage two weeks earlier!

We prayed some more just to make sure. After getting confirmation, we met with the man and gave him a check for the amount needed to build the orphanage. After the last time God had told me to give and I had delayed, costing myself twenty thousand dollars, I didn't want to postpone it this time and lose even more now that the numbers were so much higher and God had so clearly warned me.

I assumed that we would now use most of what was left to pay toward our current home mortgage. But the very same day we wrote the check for the orphanage, the Lord told me we were to invest the remainder in two specific investments. He even told Lori and me both the same amounts of how we were to split up the money between the two investments. Although we haven't cashed those investments out yet, I can tell you that as of right now, those two investments have more than doubled in value. I can also tell you that if we were to cash out right now, amazing as it sounds, we would have already made back all the money we gave to build the orphanage. Please understand I am not sharing this fact to boast but to give an example of how faithful and amazing God is! When we are obedient to what He has asked us to do, even if it is scary or doesn't make sense to us, He will take care of us and bless us in many ways.

As time went on, the Lord continued to show Himself faithful month after month with our finances, and my anxiety level slowly began to go down with this aspect of being in full-time ministry.

God's Call Confirmed

The other area that I struggled with a lack of assurance, or confidence about, was that God could use someone like me for effective ministry. I knew how many shortcomings and downfalls I had, and it just didn't make sense that He would pick me to be a minister. I didn't feel worthy enough to represent Him and definitely didn't believe I could adequately do the job or do it well enough to make a difference.

The Lord began to give me many dreams that spoke into this problem. In one dream I was taking some very nasty, foul-smelling "garbage" bags out of my "house," and then I went to my "neighbor's house" to help them get rid of some of their unpleasant, rotten "garbage." Instead of taking the garbage to the end of the driveway to get picked as most people do, I carried the garbage bags to the end of a dock that went out into a river. I then stood back and watched as a huge tidal wave of clear blue "water" came down the river and washed every trace of the "garbage" away.

This was clearly the Lord showing me that after I got rid of the "garbage" in my life, He would use me to help other people get rid of the "garbage" in their life. Jesus called Himself the "living water," and the Bible says that He was sent to take away the sins of the world, so this is obviously what the tidal wave that washed the "garbage" away stood for.

Another dream I had was of a huge vertical net out in the ocean that had buoys on the top edge and weights on the bottom edge. It went for miles in both directions, so far that I couldn't see either end. When I awoke, the Lord spoke to me and simply said, "I have made you a fisher of men." Again the Lord was reassuring me of what He had called me to do.

I began to pray and ask the Lord what the ministry would be like when it really got going and what kind of impact it would have. One night the Lord showed me a map of the world, and each continent was dark except for a very visible rainbow-colored stripe that went around the perimeter of every single landmass. When I awoke, I asked the Lord for the interpretation of the dream. He reminded me that the rainbow stood for a promise in the Bible (Gen. 9:12–17). The Holy Spirit then impressed upon me that God was making a "promise" to me that this ministry would touch every single continent of the world. Months later I was on a major international TV show that was shown on every continent. This was the beginning of God's promise to me coming true.

One Good Friday we watched *The Passion of the Christ* movie as a family, and I was very moved by it. The scope and influence of our ministry was rapidly growing, and I wanted to make sure that because of the great price Jesus paid for me, I was doing whatever He wanted me to do. When I went to bed that night, I asked the Lord to give me a dream or vision showing me what He wanted from me.

I woke up several times that night and prayed in desperation each time, but I wasn't getting anything from God. Finally one time I called out, "Lord, please show me what You want me to do." I was instantly given the vision of standing next to a beautiful stone wall holding a large paint brush. I had a bucket of what looked like white paint I was applying to the stone wall, but instead of making it white, it looked soapy instead.

I stood back and looked at the area I had just painted and watched as the liquid "affected" the wall and then dried. The area I had just worked on now gleamed and glistened compared to the surrounding areas. I asked the Lord what it meant, and He told me the "stone wall" stood for the living stones that make up the church body and the white solution was the pure truth. I was to apply the pure truth to the church, and it would wash, rejuvenate, and revitalize the people. I was to help prepare the bride for the Groom. I now realized the wall was much bigger than I had noticed and was in sections. The Lord said I was to apply the truth one section, or one church or geographical area, at a time. This simple vision gave me the direction I had asked for, but I continued to pray to the Lord for more guidance.

Commissioned by Jesus

In November 2009 I was on a short trip ministering in the rural midwest part of the United States. I spoke at four different locations in three states in three days. The night services all went for several hours as we watched the Lord save, heal, and deliver people during the prayer time. Because of having to travel from state to state in between the services and because of the long service times, by the start of the fourth service I was physically tired.

Not only that, but also each of the first three services all had something or another go wrong at them, and I was feeling quite discouraged. When I got to the last place, I went into the church to prepare for the service and asked one of the elders if the pastor was there yet. He told me that the pastor was not coming, which seemed odd, as usually the first time I speak at a church the pastor is always there.

I found out that the pastor was not there because he was not in favor of having me speak at the church. He didn't believe God still talks to people today through the Holy Spirit or heals people today, and because my testimony hinges on both those things, he was against it. One of the leaders at the church had arranged the meeting as a community event, and although the pastor didn't like it, he allowed it because this leader was very influential in the church and community.

This felt like the last straw, and I couldn't wait for this trip to be over so I could just go home. Since being in the ministry I had never had a string of services where I felt so beat up. I might have one meeting here or there that didn't go exactly the way I wanted it to, but to have four in a row and to have it be all big things was just too much.

I gave my testimony, and at the end of the service I called people forward for prayer. This was a denominational church that never did this sort of thing, so it was something out of the norm for them, and they were unaccustomed to it. A few people did come forward, who I found out later were mostly all visitors from other churches. As I was about to start praying over them individually, the Holy Spirit told me to stop. He wanted somebody else do the praying. When I asked the Lord who it was, He pointed out a man in the back row of the church. I called him forward and asked him to pray.

This church was in a very small town in the heart of the rural Midwest. I hadn't realized it up until that exact moment, but every single person in the church was white except for the man I had just called forward to pray, who was black. As it turns out, he was not from that town! As he began to pray for the people, the Lord started to give him very accurate words of knowledge. It was clear God was not only powerfully using him but also making a statement about racial issues even in churches! After the first people who had come forward had been prayed for, I invited people to the front for prayer again, but nobody else would come.

I closed the service and said that people were free to leave at that time. I made the offer again that anyone who still had prayer needs or was hungry for more of God should stay because I believed that the Lord wanted to do something in this church. Immediately over half of the people got up and left. I asked the Lord what He wanted me to do now. He told me to bring a chair to the front of the church and put it between the front two pews in the middle of the isle.

After getting the chair in place, the Lord had me call forward anyone who struggled with back pain. It took some convincing, but I was eventually able to get a group of about fifteen people to come forward and get in line behind the chair. I explained how after the accident the doctors told me I would never be able to lift anything heavier than ten pounds for the rest of my life because of the muscle and vertebrae damage I had sustained.

Sometime after the accident, while I was supposed to be on bed rest, my wife left to go get groceries and I snuck out to my garage and began to sweep the floor. There were some leaves under my Harley, and when I tried to move it, my back gave out and I could no longer feel anything but a burning sensation in the lower half of my body. I literally had to crawl to the door and wait for my wife to get back.

When she got home, she wanted to take me to the emergency room immediately, but I convinced her to help me into our bedroom instead. I called Bruce Carlson, the man who had prayed over me when my intestines grew out, and asked him to pray again. He told me to get into a chair and have Lori hold my legs out parallel with the floor. He said that one or the other of my legs would look longer at the heel than the other and that she was to command the short leg to come out in the name of Jesus and then command my back to be completely healed in the name of Jesus.

When she did, I was healed instantly! Not only did the burning and numbness go away, but all the strength in my back returned as well. In fact, the doctors ended up later removing the ten-pound weight limit they told me was going to be permanent when they found my back was completely restored.

I declared to the people that if God would do it for me, He would do it for them as well. I asked the first person in line from the group with back pain to sit down in the chair. I held out her legs as Lori had done for me and commanded the short leg to come out and the back to be healed in the name of Jesus. She was immediately healed and began to praise God excitedly.

I then had the next person in line sit down in the chair, but instead of me praying for them, I had the woman who had just been healed pray. Again, this next person was healed instantly, and now they both began to praise God loudly.

Some more of the people in the crowd got up and left at this point, but the ones who remained came forward so they could see what was happening with their own eyes. As each person prayed for the next person and the Lord continued to heal them, more and more of the approximately thirty people who were left in the church began to get excited and praise God loudly. Before long the whole group was joyfully rejoicing and glorifying God! I was told by some of the people later that in all their years going to that church, nothing like this had ever taken place before.

The Holy Spirit had led me off to the right side of the church away from the group almost as soon as I had them start praying for each other. At some point in time someone had cut a large hole in the wall of the church on that side and built a small space off of the wall that was just big enough to house the piano. They had also removed the front pew on that side of the church and had put a section of it against the back wall of this small addition, behind the piano.

I was pacing back and forth near that opening in the wall while praying by myself when all of a sudden the Holy Spirit told me to go into that little piano room. As soon as I stepped over the threshold, I instantly had a vision of Jesus sitting at the pew behind the piano! Although I couldn't see Him clearly because He was engulfed in light, every molecule in my body instinctively knew it was Him. Without thinking I immediately found myself on the floor in a posture of worship with my forehead on the carpet.

At once He said, "No, come sit next to Me." I obediently got up off of the floor and sat next to Him on the pew. We were now both looking across the top of the piano toward the group of people who were loudly rejoicing and praising God at the front of the church. He took His right hand and pointed at the group and said, "You see that. They don't even realize you're gone." His comment momentarily hurt a little, but then He let me know it made Him happy. It was exactly what He wanted: everyday people praying for each other and giving God all the glory. He continued to point at the group and then said, "That is what I want you to do: go into places and start fires in people's hearts for God, and I'll do the rest." He repeated that this made Him happy and that when I left an area, the Holy Spirit would continue to work in people's lives in the same way that a small spark is able to start a fire that burns out of control. He ended with these words before vanishing: "They don't need a superstar evangelist; they need the truth. I want to answer their prayers."

I came out of the piano room astonished at what had just happened. The deep discouragement I felt at the beginning of the service was a distant memory. Then the Holy Spirit reminded me it was less than an hour from the third anniversary of my accident. I had completely forgotten what the date was. It amazed me to think about how much had changed in three years: from a prognosis of death back to good health, from a mechanic to a minister, and from fear to faith.

It took quite a while for me to process what happened that night. In fact, the next day while driving the seven-hour trip home, I cried uncontrollably for several hours as the power and presence of God kept filling the car over and over as I pondered the previous night's events. I kept gratefully thanking Him. Although I couldn't see the Lord as I had the night before, I could still feel Him, and I knew He was there. I realized that whether I saw Him or not made no difference, and His promise to never leave us or forsake us took on new meaning for me (Heb. 13:5).

I soon recognized that after that night, the way I thought about some other things had changed also. For one, my constant questioning if God could use me and what He wanted from me in this ministry was quelled and finally put to rest. I had a newfound faith in my calling and what I was supposed to do.

The other major thing Lori and I noticed was that our constant struggle with finances immediately began to go away! For instance, within a very short time of Jesus showing up at that church, the hospital ended up canceling our enormous debt to them completely, which is almost unheard of. The offerings coming into the ministry also began to increase over the next few months to the point that we were able to take a salary that would cover our personal bills, so we no longer had to wonder where the money we needed was going to come from.

God Is Our Provider, Sustainer, and Director

To review, in the first two years after the accident we depleted all of our financial resources except for the commercial land we owned. In early 2009 we sold that land and the Lord had us donate much of the money to build the orphanage. We then invested the rest of that money as directed by God where it was no longer liquid and we had no way to use it or access it. The Lord then told us to begin to take a small monthly salary from the ministry. It wasn't enough to pay our personal monthly bills, but the Lord promised He would provide for us month by month. We did this, and somehow each month He would miraculously supply our needs. We never asked anybody for money or had to borrow any money to pay our bills either. Then finally in our fourth year of ministry, soon after having the encounter with Jesus, we began to get a salary that could support us.

As I look back now, I can clearly see that when it came to acquiring faith for finances, I had to be taken to the place where there was no plan B and no safety net. At the point that there were no reserves left and no other places to turn, I was forced to release the role of being the provider for my family to God. Submitting the responsibility to Him meant that each day, week, and month would have to be a walk of faith, believing He would sovereignly supply for my family. This is actually something He wants all people, especially all Christians, to understand. He is our provider and the only true source of everything we need and have.

God did not cause my financial problems, just as He isn't the cause of any economic crisis you might have had. He was able to use this situation in my life to teach me I could trust Him, and that lesson is more valuable than any earthly possession could ever be. We watched our faith incrementally grow as we prayed for daily provision and the Lord always came through. The building of this faith or trust wasn't limited to our finances, but it carried over into every area of our life, including what God had called us to do.

I still had my equipment and tooling, so when I got physically well enough, I could have gone back to my business. The Lord had made it very clear that He wanted me to no longer be a mechanic and that I was to work only for Him now. There were those in our life who didn't understand or agree with this, but we knew what the Lord had told us. Let me say this isn't something He calls all people to do; in fact, most Christians are called to serve God right in whatever vocation they are already in. It was because of the specific call on my life and because I had some deep-seated trust issues the Lord needed to purge from me that I was required to go on this radical walk of faith.

Each person, including you, has a call on their life from God. When you ask Him to guide you into it and show you what it is, He will, just as He did for me. Sometimes we go through discouraging times and hardships while doing what we are supposed to, but we can believe God and always be assured that when the Lord says He is with us always, He means it, whether we can see Him or not (Matt. 28:20)!

Part Two

The Five Weapons for Supernatural Victory

Part Two

The Five Weapons for Supernatural Victory

W HILE IN THE planning stages of this book in early 2010, I knew it was to be full of testimonies. I sought the Lord's guidance as to exactly what context they were to be in and how He wanted them presented.

One day at church a friend named Earl walked up and said that over the last few weeks, every time he prayed for me and the ministry he kept hearing the number five. He said he had hesitated to say anything because it seemed so insignificant, but now each time he saw me he felt convicted by the Holy Spirit for not telling me. I asked if the Lord had given him anything else with it. He said no. He was just glad that at least it was now off of his chest. He felt relieved, even if it didn't make sense to him.

While he was still standing there, another friend of mine whose name is Todd walked up to us. Todd sometimes travels with me while I'm on the road ministering, and I know that he spends several hours a day in prayer. He said the Lord had given him a word for me that morning from the account of David and Goliath, and it had to do with the number five!

Earl immediately began to tear up as he now knew he had heard the Lord correctly—and had done what he was supposed to do. (Now would be a good time for you to read 1 Samuel 17:1–51.)

The Lord told Todd to remind me that He had David pick up five stones from the brook, but David used only one to kill the giant. He also reminded me that David ended up facing five different giants in his life. Todd then reached in his pocket and pulled out a small bag with five stones in it and handed it to me. The Lord told him he was supposed to give them to me as they represented some very important truths, and if I would seek Him on it, He would reveal them to me.

I prayed and fasted over the following days, and that is when the Lord gave me the outline and main message for this book. God began to show me some prophetic truths from the narrative of David and Goliath and from David's life that I had never seen before. He also showed me how the five main miracles that have happened in my own life are an illustration of these truths. It always fascinates me that no matter how many times we may have studied a portion of Scripture, the Lord can always reveal something new to us from it. There are many "layers of truth" in the words of the Bible.

Five Stones = Five Weapons

The next five chapters are going to focus on the five key weapons God gives us to fight with as represented by the five stones David picked up from the stream. These are weapons that will release the power of God in your life and your struggles! As you read, you will get to see what they look like in action through several amazing real-life testimonies.

Just like in any battle, the weapons are only effective if used. That means if you choose not to believe God's promises and choose to be a bystander instead of a true warrior, the weapons of God will be of little value to you. If this is the case, you can count on losing many battles with the enemy and feeling discouraged more than not.

But if you, like David, choose to be a warrior and believe in God's faithfulness, then you can know what it means to be "more than a conqueror" as Romans 8:37 declares! Remember it is His power and strength that we rely on, not ours, so we don't have to be afraid.

David knew that as an Israelite he was in a covenant with God, and for this reason he trusted Him. If you are a Christian, you are also in a covenant with the living God, but your covenant is even better than David's, because it is a covenant of grace and not law.

After doing some research, I found it stated in a few places that the number five stands for grace in the Bible. Grace is much more than unmerited favor and the forgiveness of sins leading to salvation. In 2 Corinthians 12:9 Jesus Himself says that grace is His power for us. From this verse as well as others we see that grace is what God uses to empower His people (Acts 4:30–33).

In 1 Samuel 17:40 we read that David chose five smooth stones from the stream. It is clear that all of his actions that day were led by the Lord, so this was no coincidence. It speaks of God's grace or empowerment upon David, and it is prophetic of what is available to all believers! This should excite you when you realize that God wants to empower you to slay the giants in your life!

As I was praying and fasting about this, the Lord showed me that those five stones represent a complete arsenal of weapons He wants to empower us with. He knew we would be engaged in a war against giants in this life. He also knew we would need an assortment of weapons in order to be victorious. Just like soldiers in an army today sometimes might need a short- or long-range weapon—one for hand-to-hand combat, or one for battle by sea, and so on—we too need a variety of weapons in order to fight effectively.

It would be impossible to go to a stream and pick up five identical stones, so the stones David picked up that day were not the same. Although probably very similar, they would have been of varying shapes, colors, and sizes—representing the different tools the Lord gives us to fight with. The only thing the Bible says about them is that they were all smooth. We know that stones are smooth in a stream because the moving water in combination with the abrasive surroundings have shaped them that way over time. This too is prophetic as the smooth stones represent weapons that God, the living water, has shaped for us over time in this world's abrasive environment.

Second Corinthians 2:11 states that we are not unaware of the devil's schemes. In other words, we can learn from the Bible how Satan operates and what his tactics are. One of the things we see is that he wants to be like God and will often try to mimic or copy God (2 Cor. 11:13–15). For this reason he has five main tools he uses against us that correspond to the five weapons we have from God. We will see how each of the weapons God gives us is designed to defeat the opposing tool of the enemy. Neither list is meant to be an exhaustive inventory, but we will only discuss what appear to be the main ones utilized.

Divine Weapons

When David triumphed over Goliath, he didn't use a sword or a spear as expected or normal for battle in that time. God wanted everyone to know it is He who saves. Second Corinthians 10:4 says, "The weapons we fight with are not the weapons of the world. On the contrary, they have divine power to demolish strongholds." So again we see this theme of God empowering His people with unearthly weapons that will demolish the giants in their lives and the lives of others.

We must remember who we are really fighting against as we face struggles in this world. Ephesians 6:10–18 tells us we are not fighting against flesh and blood but against a hierarchy of evil forces that are sent to oppose us as long as we are on this earth. This means that we will have to be intentional about fighting the "good fight of faith" (1 Tim. 1:18–19).

But here is the great news: we are told in Colossians 2:15 that Jesus disarmed our enemies! As persistent and daunting as they may be at times, we need to remember that God gave us the weapons and took theirs away. The devil and his cohorts may have schemes and tactics, but they don't have weapons.

The Lord says in Hosea 4:6, "My people are destroyed from lack of knowledge." The living God wants us to know what these divine, unearthly weapons He has provided for us are, so that we can live a victorious life and not be destroyed by the predictable tactics of the enemy!

As Ephesians 6:10–11 says, we are to be strong in the Lord and in His mighty power, so that we can take our stand against the devil's schemes.

Supernatural victory is yours because you have been issued weapons that will release the power of God in your life!

Chapter 6

The Work of the Word

Demons Cast Out and Deception Demolished

I N OUR FIRST year of official ministry I received a crisis call early one morning from a pastor at a local denominational church. He asked if I would go with him on an emergency visit to the house of some people who believed evil spirits were harassing them. These people had just accepted Jesus into their hearts and had only attended church a few times as new believers. The pastor said he had not had a lot of experience with this type of phenomenon, but from what the couple had explained to him, he felt it was some kind of spiritual assault.

They had recently begun to hear strange noises in their house as if there were other people present, but there weren't. They experienced everything from doors opening and closing to hearing footsteps to having lights turned on and off and even other occurrences. But the worst thing wasn't the physical manifestations; it was the strong presence of evil they could feel accompanying these incidents.

The night before they called, matters had gone to whole a new level. Instead of just hearing and seeing things, they both felt physically attacked as the events in their house climaxed. First the husband felt like he had literally been touched by something evil and immediately got a very bad headache and felt sick to his stomach. They both became extremely scared, so the wife opened her Bible and just began to read it aloud for comfort. The place she "coincidentally" started reading from was where Jesus was casting out a demon. As she read the account aloud, her husband instantly got better.

The woman then began to journal the things that were happening. As she did, she felt an evil presence begin to press down on her chest so hard she had trouble breathing. At this point they became scared enough that they ran out of the house and went into a shop they have on their property and spent the night out there. They then called for help early the next morning.

When we arrived, they were both pretty shook up as they weren't sure what was happening or why it was happening. The woman was still feeling pressure on her chest. I tried comforting them by letting them know this wasn't the first time I had seen this sort of thing and that we would pray over them and the house and everything would be fine. Because they were new believers, I thought it would be best if I gave them a little bit of teaching and instruction out of the Bible before we prayed. I wanted them to know what was going on, what we were going to do, and why it would work.

I took out a small piece of paper I had in my Bible that has about twenty different verses listed on it. (I had put this list of verses together a few years earlier for another situation just like this one.) I started at the top and began to read the verses aloud one at a time and then gave a brief explanation for each verse. When I read the sixth verse on the list—John 8:36, "So if the Son sets you free, you will be free indeed"—an amazing thing occurred. The woman gasped loudly and began to swoon as if she were going to faint.

I asked her what had happened. She said that when I read the verse, she felt like she had been hit by lightning. Immediately the pressure on her chest was gone, and she could now breathe normally again. She went on to say she felt so light it was as if she could literally float away. The fear had left both of them instantly. They were now relaxed and peaceful as they realized they had only been deceived into believing the lie that they needed to fear the enemy. The truth had set them free!

To be honest, at that moment, I was quite caught off guard by what had transpired. In all of my previous experiences with breaking off demonic oppression, it had always been accomplished with much prayer and sometimes even fasting. This time it was simply achieved by reading the Bible aloud. First it happened when the wife read the Bible and her husband received immediate relief. Then it happened again when I read the verses aloud and she was instantly delivered.

What the Lord was clearly showing us in both of these instances was that the Word of God is a weapon—and not just any old weapon but a powerful one!

Clues From the Bible

As I began to study this concept in the Bible, I realized I had somehow unknowingly minimized or downplayed the true power that is in the Word of God. I knew that from its verses God tells us about Himself and what we can expect in this life as well as gives us direction and guidance. I believed every word to be true and have the ability to impart wisdom to those who followed its precepts and teachings. I also would have gone so far as to say the Word of God has to be the final authority of anything that goes on in our life, but I didn't realize the potential or capability it has to be used as a genuine "weapon" in our daily struggles.

Most Christians know or have been told we are to use Jesus as our main example of how to live our lives; in other words, we are to emulate Him. Most Christians have also read or been told about Jesus being tempted by the devil and how He answered each invitation with the phrase "It is written" before quoting verses from the Scriptures. But how many of us Christians can honestly say that when we are being tempted we quote Bible verses aloud as an answer to the temptation? How many of us are actually using the Word as a weapon?

Ephesians 6:17 says the sword of the Spirit is the Word of God. Take note: it doesn't say it is *like* a sword; it says it *is* a sword. Hebrews 4:12 gives even more detail on this: "For the word of God is living and active. Sharper than any double-edged sword, it penetrates even to dividing soul and spirit, joints and marrow; it judges the thoughts and attitudes of the heart."

We need to understand that when this verse says the Word of God is "living and active," and in another translation "living and powerful" (NKJV), it is not an exaggeration. In fact, John 1:14 declares, "The Word became flesh and made his dwelling among us." This verse speaks of Jesus. Throughout the first chapter of John Jesus is literally called the Word, showing that He is the perfect example and personification of God's message or word to us. The verses and words found in the Bible are able to take on the very nature of God because they are from God and of God. Once we begin to think and believe along these terms, the Bible will change from just being an instruction manual to being something much more powerful.

Powerful Results

One night after speaking at a church in another state, I called people forward for prayer. So many people came forward that we split the group into two lines, one on each side of the sanctuary. I had brought my friend Todd along on that trip, so I had him minister to the group on the left side of the church while I ministered to the group on the right side.

We had been praying for people for over an hour when all of a sudden the Holy Spirit told me to stop praying and go back up on the platform and stand behind the podium again. At this point over half of the people who had come forward for prayer were still waiting in the lines, but I obediently stopped praying and went back to the podium. When I got there, the Lord told me to read Isaiah 61:1–3.

After I read it, the Holy Spirit said to reread just the first sentence of verse 3, but this time start by saying, "Thus saith the Lord, 'I will...'" So this is what the people heard: "Thus saith the Lord, 'I will provide for those who grieve in Zion, to bestow on them a crown of beauty instead of ashes, the oil of gladness instead of mourning, and a garment of praise instead of a spirit of despair.'"

Standing behind the podium I had placed each one of my hands on the outside edge of my open Bible while reading from it. As I read verse 3 the second time, something incredible happened. It felt as if my Bible had become an active volcano, but instead of spewing out lava and smoke, it was emitting pure power, and that power went into my hands and up my arms and came out of my mouth as I spoke the Word.

As I declared the Word of God, I watched as the woman my friend Todd was praying for right then was thrown backward over the end of the pew and ended up on the floor like she had been hit by a prizefighter. Todd had been facing her, and he was almost knocked to the ground also, except he caught himself on the pew so that he didn't fall on top of her. It was pretty shocking to see because this was no small woman, and Todd isn't a little guy either.

Later, after the service, I found out the rest of the story. Todd said the Lord had been moving powerfully as he prayed, and he had been able to make good progress going through the line of people until he had gotten to this particular woman. She had come forward wanting prayer for depression, but each time he prayed for her, she just kept softly crying and was not able to receive the deliverance God had for her. He continued to pray and minister to her with no change, until the Lord had me go back to the front and read those verses that were obviously just for her, although I didn't know it at the time.

I had been so involved and preoccupied with praying for the people in my line that I hadn't been looking over at him. We were far enough apart that I didn't know what was going on, but God did. The Lord had me speak out and declare His Word so that the woman would be set free. (Just take a moment and reread that verse to see what the Lord has to say about depression and sorrow.)

Todd said that when the wave of God's power came at them from the platform, he felt as if he had been hit with high-voltage electricity from behind. When it came out of him and hit her, it seemed as though it had been multiplied or magnified. This energy caused her to be forcefully thrown backward over the end of the pew. She stayed on the ground several minutes in what looked like an unconscious state, but when she came to, she was no longer crying or depressed. She had been miraculously set free from all sorrow and despair.

God's Word is a powerful weapon!

God's Word Does Not Return Void

The Lord tells us about the effectiveness of His Word in Isaiah 55:10–11:

> As the rain and snow come down from heaven, and do not
> return to it without watering the earth and making it bud
> and flourish, so that it yields seed for the sower and bread
> for the eater, so is my word that goes out from my mouth:
> It will not return to me empty, but will accomplish what I
> desire and achieve the purpose for which I sent it.

We see from these verses the Lord declaring that when His Word goes forth, it will accomplish whatever He wants done and will achieve the purposes He sent it for. Sometimes those results are instant ("bread for the eater"), like the woman you just read about who was delivered from depression or the first couple at the beginning of the chapter who were liberated from the demonic oppression in their home and bodies.

Then there are those times when the desired results don't come until the word has been planted like seed and after a season it then comes to fruition ("seed for the sower"). Jesus Himself taught a parable where He used the analogy of the Word of God being compared to seeds, and the different types of soil represented the different responses people would and could have to the Word of God (Luke 8:4–15). This parable shows not only the importance of sowing the seed (the Word of God) in our hearts and the hearts of others but also the reality that because of free will we each have a choice as to what effect it will have on us.

You read in chapter 1 how, after being molested, I went to a Sunday school class and heard the story from the Bible of Jesus hugging and loving the children (the seed). Then months later I called out to Him because of that story, and He came and hugged me and poured out His love on me. This is a great example of how the Word of God was planted like seeds and how those seeds came to fruition over time, defeating what the enemy was trying to do.

Farmers know they have to plant seed in the springtime in order to enjoy a harvest later on. It would be ridiculous for a farmer to not plant seed and still expect to reap a plentiful harvest. But yet that is exactly what many Christians unknowingly do by not spending time planting the seeds of God's Word in their heart and then wondering why the enemy is able to defeat them so easily.

When Jesus was being tempted by the devil, He didn't have time to go look up verses in the Scriptures. He had those verses memorized, planted deep down in His heart, so when the "giant" came running at Him, He could reach into His bag and pull out that "stone" and defeat the enemy just as David did. If Jesus needed to have the Word of God planted in His heart like seeds so He could defeat the lies of the enemy, how much more do we?

Deception Is Demolished

As we have seen, one of the five main weapons the Lord gives us to fight with is His Word. It is the pure truth. This weapon of God is designed to directly combat one of the devil's main tactics, which is deception or lies. Jesus said in John 8:44 of the devil, "When he lies, he speaks his native language, for he is a liar and the father of lies."

If we don't know what the truth is, as stated in God's Word, we can be easily deceived. This is why the Lord said in Hosea 4:6, "My people are destroyed from lack of knowledge." This shows us why it is so important for believers to spend time planting those seeds of God's Word in their heart. It teaches us truth, which will eliminate the spiritual ignorance the devil is so good at capitalizing upon.

If you have been a believer for a while, you can probably look back on your life and see many times where this weapon of the Word has been used to bring victory in a situation without even realizing it. Once we begin to comprehend and appreciate the true power that is contained in the Word of God and start making intentional decisions to use it as the mighty weapon it is, those victories will grow exponentially!

Since discovering this truth I can't even tell you how many times we have seen people saved, healed, delivered, and supernaturally strengthened from just simply declaring the Word of God. If He will do it for them, He will do it for you!

Chapter 7

The Power of Praise

Tumors Vanished and Despair Defeated

A FEW YEARS INTO the ministry I was asked to be a part of a thirty-nine-hour healing event a pastor was holding at his church in the Midwest. He felt we were to start on a Friday afternoon and go until the early hours of Sunday morning. There was to be a constant flow of prayer and worship music throughout the entire thirty-nine hours. In order to accomplish that, he had scheduled various musicians and prayer warriors in shifts. Meals were provided at the church, and people who attended were told they could stay the entire time and even sleep right at the church if they chose.

Every hour on the hour we corporately prayed and then invited people forward and prayed for their healing. We had hoped that as the event went on, the anointing or presence of God would continue to progressively grow, but it seemed as though we were plowing through some very hard ground. We saw God touch and heal many people, but nothing really spectacular happened until about the twenty-ninth hour, which was at about 7:00 p.m. Saturday night.

The pastor got up and led that hour's corporate prayer and then spoke for a bit before calling people forward so we could pray for them one on one. While he was speaking, the Holy Spirit asked me the question, "How much glory or praise would you give Me for each miracle?" That question kept going through my mind and heart even as the pastor finished speaking and called people to the front for prayer.

About that time the woman who had been playing at the piano almost the whole day switched gears and began to play a different type of music. She had already played many various types of arrangements, but for the first time she began to play the music from some common praise songs. There was an immediate shift in the spiritual atmosphere of the place, and I could see some of the people in the seats softly mouthing the words to these popular songs as the music was played. My friend Todd was there ministering with me. We both agreed that once she started to play the praise songs, the presence of God really started to increase.

The first person in line for prayer was a man who had a tumor in his neck that visibly stuck out. I took the small bottle of anointing oil from my pocket and wet the end of my pointer finger and then placed it lightly on the tumor. Before I could even begin to pray for the man, the tumor vanished instantly! It was the first tumor I had ever seen disappear at once. I hate to admit it, but I began to poke around in his neck with my finger trying to find where it had gone.

Before I could say anything, the man lifted his hands in the air and began to loudly praise God for his healing as tears of joy rolled down his face. He turned to the crowd and yelled out that God had just removed a tumor from his neck. I wondered how he knew for sure it was gone since he had not yet had a chance to look in a mirror or even touch his neck with his own hands, but I didn't have to wonder for long. He went on to say that the tumor was big enough it had put pressure on his throat, and he could tell it was gone because there was no longer any pressure and his neck now felt "normal" again. He also declared that the Lord had removed a load of despair from his heart, and he felt joy again.

The whole place began to clap and praise God loudly for a few moments, but after it died down, it didn't seem like we had thanked God enough, so I encouraged the people to continue thanking the Lord for what He had done. After a bit the clapping and praising diminished again, but it still didn't seem like we had acknowledged the Lord enough or shown Him the appreciation He deserved. Once more the Lord asked me the question He had asked right before this miracle happened: "How much glory will you give Me for each miracle?" This time it was followed with the statement: "Whatever you choose to do will determine how the rest of the evening will go."

The pastor had made the decision when planning this event to have instrumental worship music going the whole time in the background, so that when we were praying for people or even when we were at the pulpit speaking, worship music was going forth. Interestingly enough, up until this point we had not sung one single song, but I immediately knew this was exactly what the Lord wanted to happen now. I asked the pastor if we could sing a song to the Lord expressing our gratitude and giving Him praise.

Before he could answer, the man who had just had the tumor vanish from his throat said he felt strongly we were to sing "Amazing Grace." We ended up singing through the song at least three or four times. Each time we did, the presence of God just kept getting stronger.

Praise Draws in the Presence of God

We prayed for more people and saw the Lord perform more outstanding miracles. Then it was time for the next musicians to start their shift. I had invited Jay Bryan Sandifer, the worship leader from the church I attend, to come and play Saturday night, which was when we hoped the climax of the whole thirty-nine-hour event would be. He is a highly anointed worship leader and has the ability to really bring people into a place of heartfelt praise, which will always draw in the presence of God.

The timing of what had just happened before Jay started playing couldn't have been any better, and our hopes of this thing turning into a real glory time came true. We ended up worshipping and praising God for the next three and a half hours straight. With each song the power of God in the room seemed to increase.

At one point the manifest presence of God became so strong that various people around the church began to simultaneously fall out under the power wherever they were. Many of us were so overcome by the presence of God that, although we didn't fall, we didn't have the strength to stand. Some of us ended up lying prostate on the floor for a long time—and it wasn't because we were tired. If this sounds strange to you, I understand. This wasn't the type of thing I was used to seeing either.

Several people had visions and throne room experiences with God during that time, while others received healings and deliverances right where they were seated. At one point I went to pray for a woman and stood directly in front of her with my eyes closed while I prayed. All of a sudden someone walked up behind me and grabbed me by the back of my elbow and began to move me off to the side. I assumed that either the pastor or Todd must have gotten a word of knowledge for the woman and wanted me to move so they could deliver it. I opened my eyes and stepped aside, expecting to see someone standing behind me, but there was no one. At that moment the power of God hit the woman, and she fell to the floor with no one visibly touching her. Moments later I saw a man in a white robe walk past in my peripheral vision, but when I turned my head to look directly at him, he was gone. It was obviously an angel the Lord had sent.

That weekend, as well as many other times, the Lord showed me that one of the supernatural weapons He gives us is the weapon of praise. It was praise that drew in the presence of God and caused that man's tumor to vanish, just as it was a time of extended praise that caused the power of God to get so high in the room people were healed, delivered, had visions, were physically overcome by His presence, and even had encounters with angels. Before this happened God had made it clear that if we chose to really praise Him and give Him glory, the whole night would be affected.

This shouldn't surprise us, as it says in Psalm 22:3 that God "inhabits" or is "enthroned" in the praises of His people. In other words, when we worship and praise God in earnest, His manifest presence is there. This is not to be confused with His omnipresence or the truth that God is able to be everywhere at the same time.

Many Christians would agree that as they go through their day-to-day routine at work, at home, or even in the grocery store they believe that God is with them, although many times they are not able to actually perceive or feel His presence. They would also agree that somehow at the exact same time He is with other people around the world as well. This describes His omnipresence.

Then there are those times when we encounter His manifest presence to some degree or another. It is on those occasions when we can literally feel or discern Him there with us. One person might weep uncontrollably while another gets incredibly joyful. Some people might feel a certain type of physical sensation in their body like heat, tingling, or goose bumps, while another is overcome to the point of being in what would appear to be an unconscious state. Much of this depends on what God is accomplishing in the person. There are many variables that can affect what people experience when they encounter the presence of God. The ways people react to God's presence vary almost as much as people's personalities do.

God Marches Out Like a Mighty Man

In Isaiah 42:10–13 the Lord tells us that when we sing praises to Him, raise our voices to Him, sing for joy to Him, give glory to Him, or proclaim His praise, He "will march out like a mighty man, like a warrior he will stir up his zeal; with a shout he will raise the battle cry and will triumph over his enemies" (v. 13).

We must remember that God's enemies are our enemies. If He says that when we sing praises to Him He will march out like a warrior and destroy those enemies, then that makes praise a powerful weapon for us!

The Bible is full of testimonies that show this exact thing. For example, in 2 Chronicles 20:1–22 we read the story of how the Israelite nation was about to be attacked by an army that was several times bigger than theirs. King Jehoshaphat sent out singers ahead of the army. Verse 22 says that as they began to sing and praise, the Lord supernaturally delivered them. This is a perfect example of praise being used as a weapon. Verse 22 also shows the people's deliverance didn't happen *until* they started to praise God!

I can think of several times when this same sequence of events has played out for me. Once I was ministering in a tent meeting and had just led a group of people through the prayer to receive Jesus as their Lord and Savior. Afterward I invited the people forward and began to pray with them individually. As soon as I got close to one particular woman, demonic spirits manifested in her body, and she fell to the ground screaming. I had seen this many times before and knew it was simply the enemy trying to stop what God was doing and cause a distraction. The pastor who had organized the meeting came over, and together we began to command the demonic forces to be silent and go in the name of Jesus. For some reason it was not happening as quickly as it usually did or should have.

There was a worship CD softly playing at the time. I clearly heard the Lord tell me that we were to begin praising Him, so I motioned for the soundman to turn up the music. He did, but nobody was singing along with it as they were too distracted by the screaming. Most of the people in the crowd had never seen a demonic spirit manifest in a person in this way. When they heard screams come out of her that were not human sounding, they began to get concerned. Again the Lord told me that we were to begin to praise Him as a group, and about that time the person who had led worship earlier in the evening walked up.

I asked him if he would gather his band together again and begin to lead the whole assembly in a praise song because the Lord had

The Power of Praise

just told me two times in a row that was what He wanted us to do in order to set the woman free. They went back up on the platform and started to play a praise song we had sung earlier in the night. As soon as we began to sing the first line, the woman was instantly and completely delivered from demonic oppression! Just like the story about King Jehoshaphat, the deliverance didn't come *until* people began to sing praises to God.

We see this same thing is in Acts 16:16–40. We read how Paul and Silas were beaten, thrown into prison, and chained up in stocks for doing God's work. It says that at about midnight they prayed and began to sing hymns to God. When they did, the Lord supernaturally opened the doors of all the prison cells and all the prisoners' chains fell off! Again we see the weapon of praise being used to set the captives free, and in this case it was even literal! Paul and Silas could have easily chosen to become angry or depressed because of the unjust situation they were in, but they chose to praise God instead.

Despair Is Defeated

We see that one of the main tactics the devil uses against people is despair or depression, and it is a common problem in many people's lives today. The good news is that God has given us the powerful weapon of praise in order to defeat despair. Isaiah 61:3 tells us plainly that God has given us "a garment of praise instead of a spirit of despair." When we begin to praise God, the sorrow and sadness that might be in our heart will get replaced with peace and joy, and as Nehemiah 8:10 says, "The joy of the LORD is your strength."

At times even Christians have to admit they can become depressed or dejected over a situation, but they don't need to stay that way. One night I had done an evening service in a church. Because of the amount of people who wanted individual prayer, I was still praying well after midnight, but I was getting very tired. I then prayed for several people in a row who didn't get healed instantly or even appear as though God had touched them at all. As time dragged on, I became despondent and began to wish I could leave and get back to where I was staying so I could just go to bed, but there were still several people waiting to be prayed for.

The worship band had quit hours earlier, and CDs were playing for background music. As the next person came forward for prayer, the Holy Spirit told me to close my eyes and begin to worship. Right then one of my favorite praise songs started to play on the CD, and the Lord told me to sing along. I love to sing with others, but I would never want to sing out loud by myself in front of people. If you ever heard me sing, you probably wouldn't want me to either. But I was obedient, and before I knew what happened, I had completely gotten lost in praising God so much so that I had forgotten where I even was or that someone was standing in front of me waiting for me to pray for them.

When the song ended after about ten minutes, I still had my eyes closed and was standing there just soaking in the presence of God. About then the Lord reminded me that someone was in front of me waiting for prayer. I started to get slightly alarmed as I thought about what I had just done. But before I could get upset, the Lord told me to just reach out and touch the person. When I did, the man dropped to the ground completely overcome by the power of God and ended up staying there for several minutes. I instantly realized that after praising God, I was no longer depressed or even tired. Months later I heard back from the man who had hit the floor. He told us that because of what God did in him that night, he had not been the same since.

Again it is clear that God used the supernatural weapon of praise not only to defeat the despair that was trying to attack me but also to open the door for that man to be powerfully touched by the Lord. I can tell you that after doing hundreds of services around the world, all of the ones that stick out in my mind as "high-water" marks, or in other words, services that God really did something special in, each one of them had a lengthy amount of sincere praise as part of the service. I have also seen that quite commonly during the praise time of a service, the Lord will begin to sovereignly heal and deliver people as well as begin to stir the gifts of the Spirit up in people. (See 1 Corinthians 12.)

One of the Only Gifts We Can Give God

I think one of the reasons praise is such a powerful weapon is that it is one of the only things we can give God that He doesn't already have. This makes it quite valuable.

True praise has to come from the heart, and it is a freewill choice, which is something nobody can be forced into doing. Praise therefore has the ability to get to the heart issues of people. Looking back at the time God called my name in the church, we can easily see that as I began to praise God from my heart, He showed me what was inside of it. The words in that praise song caused me to realize the depths of my addictions and sin. As I gave God access to my heart through praise, it was at that point He called my name and made Himself so real to me that day.

God is calling your name as well, and He wants you to begin to praise Him from your heart so He can become a tangible presence in your life also. He says that when we praise Him, He comes. That is why praise is such a powerful weapon against our enemies! Choose this day to quit focusing on your problems, and instead begin to praise the One who is bigger than all of your problems put together, remembering that He is the only one who can do anything about those problems anyway. Once you do, you will see why David would say in Psalm 34:1 that the Lord's praise would continually or always be in his mouth and on his lips.

Chapter 8

Ageless Authority

Paralyzed Prostitute Healed and Fear Is Flattened

AFTER WE HAD given the money to build the orphanage in Honduras, I decided I wanted to go down there and see exactly how they were using the money. I also wanted to meet the children and the people who would be running it, so I bought a plane ticket. In the meantime there was a military coup d'état in Honduras that got kind of ugly, and the US government recommended that any travel to that country should be canceled.

After praying about it at length, I felt sure I was still supposed to go, and in late August 2009 I flew down there as planned. While there I was given several opportunities to minister, and we saw the Lord do many amazing things, including one of the most profound miracles I have seen.

We had walked to a mountaintop church in a remote village. After speaking to the congregation, the pastor asked if we could walk back a different way so that we could stop and pray for one of the local prostitutes who had attended that church for a time. It turned out this woman was involved in witchcraft and occult practices and kept getting into arguments with the pastor. She finally left one day after giving the pastor a death threat in front of the whole congregation. At some point soon after that she became paralyzed from just below her arms and down, and the pastor had not seen her since.

The pastor said that this woman actually had quite a bit of influence in this village, and because of the lack of police presence, there was a very real possibility the woman could have the death threat against the pastor carried out. This pastor had already seen the Lord perform many healing miracles while we were there, and although it wasn't stated directly, it seemed clear the hope was that the prostitute would be healed so the pastor wouldn't have to worry about this death threat any more.

By the time we got to her open-walled hut, we were all sweating due to the ninety-plus-degree temperature and nearly 100 percent humidity that day. The woman was lying in a homemade bed that was against the only wall in the eight-foot by eight-foot hut. We were told she had been confined to the bed for several months ever since she had become paralyzed.

As we entered the hut, the first thing that caught my attention was the horrible smell. Looking for the source of that smell, I noticed a five-gallon pail on the floor against the edge of the bed that she used for a toilet since she couldn't get up to go anywhere else. I also saw that her pullover dress and the bedding she was lying on were severely dirty and stained. We were then told that although she was confined to the bed, she was still "in business" because she needed money for food. All of this, combined with the fact there was obviously no running water for cleaning and never had been, made me feel ill and not want to get too close.

I have to admit that I am kind of "germaphobic" anyway, so this was really a stretch for me. I mustered my courage and decided it was simply mind over matter as I stood over her and talked to her through the interpreter. She was now more receptive to the gospel than she apparently had been in the past. We ended up leading her through a short salvation prayer. After that I explained through the interpreter that we were going to pray for her physical healing.

Jesus's words from Mark 16:17–18 came to mind that "those who believe...will place their hands on sick people, and they will get well," but I really didn't want to touch this woman. After a few moments I complied and decided that the safest place to touch her would be on the sides of her neck. I prayed for her and then commanded her body to be healed in the name of Jesus. I felt the power of God come down, and at that moment her crooked neck instantly straightened out and her eyes got very big as she too recognized the power of God working in her body. I quickly told the interpreter to tell her to get up and walk in the name of Jesus.

The interpreter was a young woman who had been thrown into this position with no past experience and had not seen this kind of praying before. She looked at me anxiously before she very quietly and timidly repeated what I said. I immediately repeated what I had said very loudly and boldly, "Get up and walk in the name of Jesus!" I then told the interpreter to do it the same way. To her credit she did, and the paralyzed woman stood up and was immediately healed.

The small group who had come with us to pray began to loudly praise God and clap. I quickly exited the hut in order to get some "fresh" air. I watched the woman from outside the hut and was very disappointed to see that she really didn't appear to be that happy. She kept looking down at her legs and moving them, looking fearful, almost as if she expected them to quit working again.

Authority With No Love Equals No Joy

I began to complain to God asking Him why she wasn't joyful and why she appeared fearful—after all, this was a miracle that could have been straight out of the Bible. God instantly replied and simply said a very profound statement: "She doesn't know how much I love her." Then the Lord began to remind me of times I, and others I know, hadn't been joyful or happy even though the Lord has done so many miracles for us, and we had already been told of His love.

I felt guilty for judging the woman and asked the Lord what He wanted me to do.

He said to go back in the hut and pray that the spiritual veil would be lifted from her heart and the woman would be able to receive His love and peace. I marched back in the hut and placed my hands on the side of her head and prayed. The power and love of God came down on the woman, and she collapsed on the ground. Several minutes later when she awoke, she began to cry. I was confused until the Lord explained that, because she received a revelation of the depth of His love for her, she was experiencing godly sorrow for her sins for the first time (2 Cor. 7:8–12).

At that point she went to the pastor whom she had caused so much trouble for and kept repeating over and over how sorry she was. They both cried and hugged for a long time. Finally I began to see a smile and a sense of peace and joy in the woman. The rest of the group was gathered around her and started taking turns hugging her and each other.

This made me happy, and I began to really praise God for letting me see this miracle firsthand. Then the Lord began to ask me some questions. He said, "Have I sent you to be My mouthpiece here?" and I said, "Yes, Lord." He said, "Have I sent you to be My hands and feet here?" and I said, "Yes, Lord." He then said, "Then go hug her and hug her the way I would." And I said, "No, Lord, please no."

At that moment she turned to me and gave me a big old smile that screamed, "It's your turn for a hug." Right then I did the only thing I could think of and told the interpreter to go give her a big hug, which bought me some time. While they were hugging, I devised a plan that would help me to be obedient while still allowing me not to have to smell her up close. I would just step into the hut and hug her while holding my breath. The only concern this left me with was the fact that we had already been told not to let our heads touch the people's heads because of the epidemic lice problem.

The interpreter finished hugging the woman, and I began to step into the hut for my turn after taking in a very deep breath. As I stepped in, God spoke again and said, "By the way, when Jesus reached out His hand to touch the leper, He wasn't afraid of getting leprosy." This comment cut so deeply that I literally gasped and unfortunately let out the breath I was holding.

With every inch I got closer to the woman, the horrendous smell got worse. Before I knew what I was doing, my arms were wrapped tightly around her and my right cheek touched against her cheek. At that exact moment the horrible smell was gone. As silly as this sounds, I began to forcefully sniff, trying to find where the smell went.

I asked the Lord why I couldn't smell her bad odor anymore. He said, "Because you are now smelling her with My nose." After letting me consider this profound statement for a moment, He continued, "By the way, you're smelly too, because it is sin that makes people stinky. But when they repent, it goes away." I immediately repented of my sinful, selfish attitude and asked the Lord to forgive me for not really loving this woman the way He wanted me to.

Every time I tell this story people end up laughing like crazy, but for the first few years after it happened, I couldn't tell it without breaking down and crying. God has given us the weapon of authority, but it has to be tempered and used with love, otherwise it has little lasting value (1 Cor. 13). The authority God gives us should always make us think about His love and end up driving fear away.

The Weapon of Authority

It is absolutely clear from the Bible that one of the main weapons the Lord gives us to fight with is the weapon of authority, although this may be one of the least used and least understood concepts in the church today. When we commanded the woman to rise up and walk in the name of Jesus, it was using the authority that we have been given by Jesus and through the name of Jesus that caused her to be healed. After Peter and John ordered a crippled man to rise up and walk in the name of Jesus and he was healed, the religious leaders wanted to know how they did it. Peter answered them in Acts 4:10, "Then know this, you and all the people of Israel: It is by the name of Jesus Christ of Nazareth...that this man stands before you healed."

In Matthew 28:18 Jesus declared that *all* authority had been given to Him. In Luke 10:19 He says that He has given *us* the authority over *all* the power of the enemy. But what does that look like in day-to-day life?

He tells us in Mark 11:22–23 to speak to the mountain, and throughout His ministry He gives us plenty of examples so that we would know what He meant. For instance, in Luke 4 He rebuked the fever in Peter's mother-in-law, and it left her. In Luke 8 He rebuked the wind and the waves, and they became calm. Over and over He showed us what the "mountains" were and how we were to deal directly with them at times. After all, the Bible says that we are made in the image of God, and He spoke the whole world into being (Gen. 1). This makes our spoken declarations powerful whether we realize it or not!

I explained in chapter 3 how I was lying in the hospital and wasting away because I didn't have enough intestines left after the accident to sustain life. Many people had come and prayed for me in the hospital, but nothing happened until Bruce Carlson came and prayed over me. Everyone else had come in and begged God to save my life, but he showed up and spoke directly to the mountain that in my case was my intestines and commanded them to super-naturally grow back in the name of Jesus. It was only then that the creative miracle instantly happened.

As I travel around in ministry and pray for people in this manner myself, I sometimes interact with people who are unfamiliar with the concept of authority and what it looks like in prayer. I will often explain that it is not out of arrogance or presumption that we pray this way, but out of obedience as Jesus told us to speak to the mountain.

One night early in the ministry I was trying to teach some people how to pray for one another in this church, and we weren't having very good results because they didn't want to pray the way I was telling them to. They were uncomfortable with the way I prayed because they had been taught that if they prayed for someone, they were to always add at the end of the prayer "but only if it is Your will, God." So because of that they didn't want to speak to the problem and command it to go. We went back and forth, and I finally asked them if their way worked so well, why had they already told me that they had never seen God do any miracles before? They didn't have an answer to that but still couldn't understand what I was saying.

All of a sudden the Lord gave me an analogy I could use to show them how authority worked. I said, "Let's say it's a hundred years ago, I am the mayor here in your town, and I need to hire a new sheriff. After he is hired, I give him his badge and a six-shooter pistol and send him out. A few days later he calls me from a bank robbery that is in progress and tells me I need to get down there and do something about it. What am I going to tell him? I am going to say, 'Look, I have given you the badge and a pistol, which stands for the authority and power you now have, and I expect you to use them. It is your job, go take care of it!'"

I also reminded them that the Bible tells us Adam and Eve lost dominion over the earth to the devil, but Jesus came and won it back and made it available to us again. When we believe in Jesus, we get the "badge" of being called a Christian, and we also get the "weapon of authority" that comes with it. He expects us to use that authority just as the mayor expects the sheriff to use the authority given to him. Very often the longer we have been Christians, the more God will require us to use that authority.

As soon as I explained it like that, they were able to grasp what I meant, and we instantly began to see people get healed as they prayed for each other in that manner. I have continued to use that analogy of the mayor and sheriff for the authority God gives us, as it really does do a good job of showing how authority is delegated. It helps further explain why Jesus said in John 20:21, "As the Father has sent me, I am sending you." It is also important to note that we never see Jesus ever beg God the Father for anything, even when He was agonizing in the garden over the horrible death He knew He was about to suffer.

We Are Not Beggars—We Are Children of God

I spoke at a church one Sunday morning, and after closing the service I invited those who wanted prayer to come forward. As I prayed for people, I noticed a husband and wife who were watching me very closely from the seats but never came to the front for prayer. When I finished praying for those present, I went to the back of the church and began to pack up the leftover items from the book table so I could leave.

After a few minutes the couple appeared with two little children in tow. The husband rather hesitantly asked if I would pray for his wife, who had severe pain in her back and shoulders from a bad injury. As soon as I stood in front of the woman and was about to pray, the Holy Spirit very clearly told me the man was to pray for his wife instead of me, so I told the husband that I felt he was to pray for his wife.

He immediately became angry and growled, "Don't you think I already have prayed for her?" I was kind of caught off guard by his response, but I gently explained to him that was what I felt the Lord had said and I wanted to just be obedient to it.

He agreed and began a very heartfelt prayer for his wife that lasted several minutes. At one point he broke down crying and began to beg God to heal his wife because of the strain this injury had put on their whole family. When he finished, the Holy Spirit told me she didn't feel one bit better. Before I could think about what I was saying, I said to the woman what I had just heard, "You don't feel one bit better, do you?" (Sometimes I'm not the smartest guy around.)

The husband clenched his fist and stepped toward me. He looked me in the eye and said, "How dare you say that to her!" I told him I had just repeated what the Holy Spirit had spoken to me. I asked his wife again if she felt better or not. She sheepishly looked at her husband and shook her head no.

I told the man to pray again, but this time he should pray the way Jesus taught us: speak to the mountain (as I had been teaching on for the last two hours). This was the final straw, and the man went off like a bomb. "Don't tell me I don't know how to pray. I've been in ministry. I attended a four-year Bible college and heard you say today that you haven't had any formal schooling for ministry. Who do you think you are?"

Before he could say anything more, I stopped him and told him to just give it a try; if it didn't work, he had nothing to lose. He looked at me with disgust and said, "How do you want me to pray?" I once again told him to speak to the mountain and tell it to leave in the name of Jesus. In this case the mountain was the pain in his wife's body.

In an almost mocking tone he placed his hands on her and said, "Pain, go in the name of Jesus." She hunched forward and shook a bit before declaring that she was now entirely pain free. As crazy as this sounds, that seemed to make him even angrier. He wanted to argue with me why God would answer a prayer like that when He didn't answer his long, sincere prayer.

I explained to him that it had nothing to do with God not answering his prayer and everything to do with using the authority he had been given to stop what the enemy was trying to do in their home. There are times when we need to get before the Lord and offer up prayers from the bottom of our heart. Then there are those times when we need to start using the weapon of authority and kick the enemy out!

He ended up setting his pride aside and getting excited enough after his wife got healed to ask for prayer for his little girl, who had an eye disease and was supposed to be blind within a few years. So we prayed for her. I was told later that at her next appointment the doctors could no longer find any sign of the disease and gave her eyes a clean bill of health. Thank You, Lord!

What Does Authority Sound Like?

One night I was preaching in the Deep South at a fairly large event. When it came time to pray for people, I noticed a family coming up through the line. It was obvious the mom and dad didn't want to come forward, but their two young children were literally dragging them to the front. When it was their turn, I asked what the prayer request was. The children answered that their mother had a bad back and hip from an accident that always caused her pain, so they wanted me to pray for her so she would get healed. They had heard me tell my testimony of physical healing that night and believed me when I declared that God would do it for others as well. Mom and dad obviously weren't as believing.

Immediately the Lord told me to have the children pray for their mother instead of me doing it, so I began to coach them how to pray. (The girl was about eleven or twelve, and the little boy was about seven or eight years old.) I told them to speak to the hip and back and command them to be healed and operate the way they were designed in the name of Jesus. When I was finally able to coax it out of them, it was barely audible, and nothing happened to the disappointment of us all.

Right then the Lord told me to ask them what kind of pet they had, although I wasn't sure why at first. They told me they had a dog. The Lord then told me the dog liked to run away and that I should ask them what they did when the dog ran away. These two quiet little children both yelled out at once, "Charlie, get home!" so loud it made people standing around us jump.

Then the Lord told me I was to tell them to speak to their mother's bad hip and back just like they were Charlie the bad dog. You should have seen those kids go to town! The pain and stiffness immediately left the mother's body, and after she stood up, she found she had full range of motion again. Needless to say, she began sobbing when she realized what God had just done, which caused the kids to begin sobbing, which left the doubting dad scratching his head as to what had just happened.

I know that God wanted to make an important statement to those people that night, but it also gave me some great insight as to what the weapon of authority sounds like. I ended up doing a word study on it in the Bible and was surprised how many times I found it recorded that people, including Jesus and His disciples, prayed loudly. In fact, it says in Hebrews 5:7, "During the days of Jesus' life on earth, He offered up prayers and petitions with loud cries and tears…and he was heard because of his reverent submission."

This must be a hidden verse in the Bible, because I have met several people who believe it is anything but reverent for people to pray loudly in church. Don't get me wrong; I don't believe that we need to always be yelling when we are praying, but I do believe there are those times when we need to use the weapon of authority, and some of those times we will need to get loud, even if we are in church.

Since that night I have seen this play out several times as I am praying over people. More than once I have prayed over someone, and when nothing happens after praying a few times, I am tempted to move on to the next person in line. The Holy Spirit then will rebuke me and tell me to "pray like I mean it." In those instances I will pray again, but much louder and with boldness, and when I do, the healing comes. Nothing changed in the situation to effect a healing, except the enemy now realized that I was serious about using the authority given to me. In other words, we need to know who we are in Christ.

What Does Authority Look Like?

I believe this is what James 5:16 describes when it says in the King James Version, "The effectual fervent prayer of a righteous man availeth much." The Greek phrase translated here as "effectual fervent" is known to describe something that is "powerful" and "has energy." As we found earlier with Jesus and others in the Bible, this can at times even mean loud.

The very next verse says that Elijah was a man just like us, and he prayed that it would not rain and it didn't rain for over three years! If you think that was made up or things like that don't happen anymore, let me tell you that I as well as many others have seen things just like this.

For example, two guys were replacing the roof on my friend Todd's house one summer. They had it all torn apart when a huge rainstorm started to blow in. As soon as Todd heard the rain starting to come down, he went out on the porch and loudly commanded it to stop raining over his house in the name of Jesus. He said you could see the rain coming down everywhere else around them, but right above his house it had stopped.

At the end of the day the two roofers came down off the roof after finishing their work and knocked on his door, wanting to talk to him. They had heard what he had done and had seen with their own eyes what had happened and how it continued to rain all around them, but not on his house. They wanted to know how or why what he did worked.

He explained to them about the power that is in the name of Jesus and the authority Christians have. He told them what they saw was that authority in action. Later Todd ended up leading them both in a prayer to accept Jesus as their Lord and Savior all because of a seed that was planted when they saw someone using the authority God gives His children. After Todd told me this testimony, I shared it with many people who in turn used the weapon of authority God gives us over even nature and had similar things happen, including in my own family.

Fear Is Flattened

One night we were driving home from a holiday get-together at my mom's house, and the fog got so bad we could not see at all. I slowed down to about ten to fifteen miles an hour, but it didn't make any difference, and we had a long way to go to get home. At one point we almost hit the back of a car that had stopped in the road. The kids then began to get a little frightened as they realized the danger of the situation.

We talked about the authority God gives us over nature, and then I asked my children who wanted to use it. My youngest daughter volunteered and then commanded the fog to go in the name of Jesus. We all watched in amazement as the fog instantly evaporated around us right on cue! Not only did the fog immediately vanish, but the fear that was trying to come on my children did as well. That is what authority looks like in the life of a believer, even in a ten-year-old little girl.

One of the biggest tactics the devil tries to use on people is fear, but God gives us the weapon of authority to flatten fear. Just think about it; it is impossible for a person to feel as though they truly have authority or power over something and still be afraid of it. I'm sure that is why Jesus made sure to tell us in Luke 10:19 that he has given us the authority ("power" in the King James Version) over all the power of the enemy. And in 2 Timothy 1:7 we read much the same thing, "For God has not given us a spirit of fear, but of power and of love and of a sound mind" (NKJV).

God has given His children power and authority and wants us to know we don't ever need to be afraid of the enemy or anything that is going on around us, but that doesn't stop the devil from trying to get us to buy into that lie. I believe that is one of the reasons why the Bible says he is like a roaring lion in 1 Peter 5:8. I have read that one of the reasons lions roar at night is to try and instill fear in other lions that might be in the same territory as well as to try and get animals they are hunting afraid enough they will run and then become easier to find.

Just remember when you hear the enemy roar in your ear in the dark, you don't have to be afraid because God has given you authority and power over him! As 1 John 4:4 says, "The one who is in you is greater than the one who is in the world."

Chapter 9

Potent Prayer

Throne Room Encounters and Pride Put Down

Abusinessman and evangelist named Doug Collins invited me up to Canada to speak at a few events over a weekend after seeing my story on television. Before going on the trip I had the chance to speak with Doug several times on the phone and found out that he was involved in much ministry himself. He had preached at several places in North America; he was also a part of some large crusades in Africa and had funded an orphanage there.

We swapped ministry stories, and I was excited with some of the astounding miracles they had seen the Lord do while on the mission fields of Africa as well as right here in North America. My hope was that even though he had invited me to come and minister there, I would be able to gain some "God-given" knowledge or insight from him as well, and I wasn't disappointed.

The first thing we did was a community event on a Friday night in Windsor. Then we did a Sunday morning church service in the Greater Toronto area. We ended the trip with a church service on that Sunday evening, also in the Greater Toronto area. Doug had introduced me at both of the first two services and I preached. When it came time for praying over the people, he helped a little, but for the most part he just let me do it and observed. After hearing of the many great things he had seen the Lord do before in the past, I was curious as to how he thought the first two services had gone, so I asked him.

He told me he thought they had been great but said he usually prayed before the services in a different way than I did. He suggested that for the last service we could do it "his" way if I wanted, and I agreed. I have to admit this confused me a little as I couldn't think of any other way to pray than the way I did, but I soon found out what he was talking about.

There was about four hours left before the last service started. We were back at the place we were staying, and he invited me to come over to his room so we could begin praying. This was a little different, as I normally will wait until the last hour to half hour before the service to get into serious prayer, and I will then pray until it starts if possible.

Once in the room he flopped down on the bed and told me I could just lie down on the thick carpet and get comfortable. I did, and then I heard him say something like, "Holy Spirit, we just invite You into this place," and that was it. After a few more minutes he said it again, and once more was quiet for several minutes before saying something like it again. "Lord, we love You. Holy Spirit, just come."

I quietly pulled out my phone and checked the time. We had been in there for nearly half an hour, and I was beginning to get a little restless. When I pray before a service, I will ask the Holy Spirit to come, but then I will begin to go through several very specific requests, petitions, and thanksgivings. I'll ask the Lord to bring people to the meeting. I'll ask Him to give me the words He wants me to say. I'll ask Him for salvations. I'll ask Him to do signs, miracles, and wonders. I'll thank Him for the opportunity to minister. I'll also thank Him for His faithfulness. I guess the point is that when I pray, most of the time I am actively doing something and focusing on me and my concerns and not just resting or waiting, courting the presence of God.

Another twenty minutes passed, and I heard Doug say, "Holy Spirit, please come." Now I know the Bible tells us that as Christians we have the Holy Spirit living inside of us. I knew that Doug believed that too, so he was obviously praying for something more than that, which was fine with me, but I didn't know how long he was willing to wait or what he was exactly waiting for. I am a pretty hyper and intense person, and I was really struggling to stay lying on the floor this long. I looked at my phone and decided I would give it ten more minutes, and then I was going to quietly get up and go back to my room. I didn't want to seem rude or offend Doug in any way, but I just couldn't handle lying there any longer and doing "nothing."

When the one-hour mark came, I was about to try and get up and sneak out of the room when I heard the Lord tell me I was to stay a while longer. A few minutes passed, and again I heard Doug softly call, "Holy Spirit, come like You did in the Bible." My eyes were closed and my mind continued to wander, and about another ten minutes passed before "it" happened.

Words can't really describe what happened exactly, but I can tell you what it kind of seemed like. First, imagine being on the edge of an ocean when there is some kind of storm or for some reason the waves are really big and they come crashing down on the beach with a lot force. Next, imagine that you were able to go lie on the beach in between the waves, and when the next wall of water came crashing down, it came down right on top of you. That is what it felt like to me.

It was sudden and unexpected, and it really did feel like a wall of water had fallen on me and had completely enveloped me to the point of even filling my lungs—so much so that it took my breath away and I found myself literally gasping for air! All of a sudden I heard Doug yell loudly, "Double portion, Lord!" Before I had time to even contemplate what was going on, it happened again. After the initial shock went away, I found myself in such a tangible presence of God that it was as though I was right at His throne and was content to just lie there and enjoy Him without feeling the need to communicate or ask for anything at all.

Time seemed to slip away, and at some point He began to give me visions of specific people who were going to be at the meeting that night. The Lord not only showed me what they looked like and what they would be wearing, but He also told me what their prayer needs were. Doug was also getting visions and "words of knowledge." We got a notebook and began to write them down so we wouldn't forget anything. That night at the meeting every single person the Lord showed us and every "word of knowledge" He gave came to pass. Please remember this whole episode took place because of prayer that focused on God alone.

The Weapon of Prayer

Probably the most well-known and discussed weapon that the Lord gives His children is the weapon of prayer. Over and over in the Bible we find that we are instructed to pray. First Thessalonians 5:17 says to "pray continually." Philippians 4:6 tells us to not be anxious about anything, but pray about everything instead.

There might be several things that Christians can find to disagree about around the world, but one of the things they always agree upon is that we should pray to God. Any differences that might arise in that subject will be about "how" people pray, as there truly are many types of prayer and ways to pray.

For example, I had prayed to God for over thirty years and had been in ministry for a few years and truly thought I had a good grasp of what personal prayer entailed before I encountered the type of prayer Doug Collins introduced me to. It was a type of prayer where the goal was to focus on God and just immerse one's self in His presence. I have since found out that it is interestingly enough referred to as "soaking" prayer in some circles, which makes me laugh because of how it actually felt like a wave of water to me when the presence of God came. We also see in the Bible where Jesus talked about the "living water" in John chapter 4, and in John 7:37–39 He again uses the term "living water" to describe the Holy Spirit, which is exactly what Doug prayed for to come.

From the Old Testament to the New Testament we see different people who engaged in extended times of prayer with God and the incredible things that often accompanied those times of prayer. In Luke 6:12 it is recorded that Jesus went out one day to pray and ended up praying through the whole night! (This was the night before He picked the twelve disciples.) We also read several other times where He went away to spend extended times of prayer with God. Considering the amounts of time He spent in prayer and that He said in Matthew 6:7–8 not to babble or use "vain repetitions" (NKJV) with many words, it would be safe to say that Jesus was a fan of what people today would call "soaking" prayer. It is truly one of the best ways we can "rest" in God's presence as it is described in Hebrews chapter 4.

We need to remember that no matter what method or type of prayer we engage in, it is a way to spend time with God and stay plugged into Him. Our ambition should be to concentrate on God and His plans above our own. His plans are far better and more successful than anything we could come up with. It is a weapon we can use anywhere and at anytime in order to help us and those we come in contact with to live a supernatural life of victory while here on this earth.

Two-Way Street

When we take a closer look at prayer in general, we find it is meant to be more than what it often turns out to be, because we have frequently made it into something it is not. It is not meant to be a monologue, a one-way transmission where we send our prayers up to God and then walk away. It is meant to be a dialogue where we are in actual communication with God, a give-and-take.

Imagine that you called your best friend on the phone. When he answered, you began to talk without ever once giving him the opportunity to respond, and when you were finished talking, you just hung up the phone. I know this sounds silly, but this is exactly how many people pray to God. They tell Him their requests and then just walk away or roll over and go to sleep without listening for Him to respond. This in itself is a form of pride as the person is so inward focused that he or she isn't listening for what God has to say. Most of the time I don't think this is done on purpose; many people just don't expect God to talk back to them.

Jesus said in John 8:47, "He who belongs to God hears what God says," and in John 10:27 He said, "My sheep listen to my voice." Just from these two verses He couldn't make it any clearer that we are supposed to be hearing Him speak to us. Let me give an example of what that can look like.

One day a woman saw me on television and then called my number and left a message with just her name and return number on it. After listening to her message, I prayed for her, and as I prayed, the Lord clearly spoke the name Robert to me. When I called her back, she said her prayer request was that she wanted to be able to feel and know God's love for her.

She went on to tell me about many of the problems she was having in her life: a struggling marriage, two children who were seriously ill, and now she had just lost her job. She also mentioned she had been adopted and was the only non-blood child in the family; while growing up, she had been physically, emotionally, and verbally abused. She then said that although she had believed in God since she was a little girl, she could never feel His love.

We started to pray, and the Lord told me to tell her He knew and loved her even when she was still in her mother's womb. I then prayed that she would be able to physically feel the love and presence of God. She said she felt a warm tingly sensation come over her whole body but admitted that it was hard to believe in her heart that God really loved her after all of the bad things she had been through in her life.

The Lord told me to ask her what the name Robert meant to her, and she said it was name of her brother. God immediately said, "No, ask her what else it means to her." So I asked her again, and this time she cried out, " Oh, my God!" She said that she had a picture of herself as a newborn baby in the hospital, and written on the plastic tub she was in was the last name of her biological mother— Robert. Someone had tried to cross it out on the picture with a pen, but she had been looking at it for years and was convinced it said Robert. Her mother had abandoned her at the hospital when she was only two days old. Ever since she was eighteen she had been trying to track down her biological parents, and all she had to go on was this picture. The laws in her state made it illegal for the hospital or anyone in the state adoption program to give out that information. At this point she had basically given up hope of ever finding her biological parents.

Think about it. This woman called asking to be able to feel and know God's love for her. So the Lord had me tell her that He knew and loved her while she was still in her mother's womb and then proved it to her by giving her the only thing she knew about her biological mother, her last name. It was something she could hang on to and believe, because only God would have known that information. I fully believe it was life changing for her even though I have never heard back from her.

The reason I shared this testimony with you is because the whole thing hinged on the power of two-way prayer with God. If I would have just prayed about what I thought was important or would have prayed and then not taken the time to listen for His answers, none of it would have transpired. Please hear me when I tell you that God wants to have that same interaction with you! There is nothing about my relationship with God or the way I hear from Him that isn't available to all believers who desire it.

Just like any other relationship, though, it does take time and intentional decisions to get to know the other party and have a healthy connection. God wants us to value His presence and truly seek Him. As I have learned, that often will take some time and even sacrifice, but it is well worth it!

Pride Is Put Down

One of the main tactics the enemy uses against people is pride. The only problem is that when someone is struggling with pride, they are the usually the last one to know it. The other sneaky thing about pride is that it can take on two completely different appearances. The common form that most people associate with pride is the one of arrogance and an overly high opinion of oneself. The other form of pride is just as real but is often harder to detect. It is when individuals believe that they are so bad or inadequate in some way or another that there is no help for them or their situation.

In both cases the focus is on self, and that is the essence of pride! God wants us to focus on Him, and that is why the mighty weapon of prayer is what God gives us to combat pride. Prayer has the ability to take the focus off of us and put it on God where it belongs. When we spend time in earnest prayer to God that comes from our heart, it is hard to focus on anything but Him.

First Peter 5:5–7 tells us, "'God opposes the proud but gives grace to the humble.' Humble yourselves, therefore, under God's mighty hand, that he may lift you up in due time. Cast all your anxiety on him because he cares for you." So we see that God says the cure for pride is to humble oneself, and the way He says to do that is to cast our cares on Him. In other words, pray!

In chapter 4 you read how I prayed almost the whole night before the Holy Spirit showed up in our bedroom and we had a Pentecost-type experience. Although I didn't realize it, I was struggling with pride at the time because I was focusing on myself and my inabilities to speak in front of people to the point that I almost didn't believe the Lord could do anything about it.

By using the mighty weapon of prayer and humbling myself before God all night, pride was finally broken when the Lord sent the Holy Spirit in power. This is just what verse 5 said: He gives grace to the humble, and as we learned earlier, His grace is His power!

I encourage you to cast your cares on the Lord through prayer and show Him you are serious, just like the persistent widow found in Luke 18:1–8 who cried out day and night. Jesus said that when we do, God will see that we get justice—and quickly! Use the weapon of prayer today, and watch your problems shrink as your perspective of God grows.

Chapter 10

The Force of Faith

Deaf Ears Opened and Doubt Destroyed

E ARLY IN OUR ministry I spoke at a church one night and then made the offer for people to come forward for prayer. One of the people who came forward that night was the secretary of the church. She had not been able to hear out of her right ear for over twenty years and felt that the Lord was nudging her to get prayer for it this night.

She informed me she had been prayed for many times before for the deaf ear, but nothing had ever happened. Any time someone makes a statement like that before I pray for them, it always disappoints me because I know we are fighting not only against the infirmity but also possibly against the unbelief that can so easily come in after several years of unanswered prayer. To make it even worse, this was a full gospel church with a pastor who fully believed in healing and actively prayed for the sick, so if she was going to get healed after prayer, this was the kind of place it was going to have happened in already.

After we prayed, she walked away with no change in her ear. I continued praying for the other people who had come forward.

The next morning the pastor called me at my house and excitedly told me the secretary had just called him and said she could now hear out of her "bad" ear. I asked him if I could have her number and call her to see what she had to say, as this was the first deaf ear I had seen get healed.

When I got her on the phone, I asked what exactly had happened after I prayed for her, and she said quite bluntly, "Nothing happened after you prayed for me. But when I went to bed, I told the Lord, 'I don't care how many times I've been prayed for and there hasn't been any change; I am not going to get disappointed this time and doubt my healing because I fully believe You have heard every one of those prayers and You are my healer.'" Then when she got up in the morning, she found she could hear out of her ear.

I contemplated and prayed about this for several days and finally came to some conclusions. I had already seen many times when I prayed for someone and the healing didn't come until later, but I knew this case was somehow different. What the Lord showed me was the same thing the woman had so clearly pointed out to me; her healing really had nothing to do with my prayer. It was actually her faith that activated the healing.

I had to be honest with myself and conclude that when I prayed for her, my faith was pretty low after she gave me her background and I felt the "odds" were not favorable. The Bible says in Hebrews 11:1, "Now faith is being sure of what we hope for and certain of what we do not see," and that definitely did not describe how I felt when praying for her. This made me really take a look at the importance of faith, not only just for the one receiving prayer but also for the one praying. I had to look at the implications of this for my personal life as well and not just in the scope of ministry.

I chose to use the lesson as a learning tool and began to pray for a revelation of faith. I also decided if God would open her deaf ear, He would do it again. About two months later I saw God open a completely deaf ear instantly and perfectly. Over the next couple of years I kept track of every time we saw the Lord open a deaf ear, even if it had only been partially deaf, and when I got to fifty, I decided to quit counting.

Because that secretary chose to believe God's promises and still stay positive and not doubt, even when it didn't appear as though anything was changing, she got healed. And because she got healed, it raised my faith so that I could believe it would happen again, and the cycle of faith just kept going and repeating. That is how faith works and will continue to spread and grow if given the opportunity.

Faith Is a Mighty Weapon

Remember our hero David? When David ran toward Goliath that day on the battlefield, he couldn't have done it without the weapon of faith. Let's face it; experienced warrior versus runt boy is about as bad of odds as you could imagine. But the Bible clearly says that David not only chose to fight Goliath, but he also ran toward him when the time came! It seemed like a suicide mission to all those watching, but David didn't think so. He gave the reason for his confidence in 1 Samuel 17:34–37. He had fought off lions and bears while watching his father's sheep. He said in verse 37, "The LORD who delivered me from the paw of the lion and the paw of the bear will deliver me from the hand of this Philistine."

David's faith in God's deliverance was based on the faithfulness of what God did in the past and the promises of God's help found in the Scriptures. We need to be like David and believe that just as God has helped us and others in the past, He will do it again. "But God has never helped me in the past," one might say. Well, even for the person who thinks this is true, we have the Bible that shows God sent Jesus to die for us. According to Romans 5:8 He did it while we were still sinners and didn't even know who He was. This act of sacrifice was the greatest thing He has done for anyone as it has the ability to affect our eternity. One of the supernatural weapons God gives us to fight with is the weapon of faith, and what is so great about that weapon is that it can become contagious. When David had the faith to fight Goliath and then won, it caused the whole Israelite army to realize they could beat the Philistines, and they did. When that church secretary had the faith to believe God would heal her deaf ear that night, her testimony has caused many other people to be healed from their deaf ears over the following years—and it hasn't stopped yet!

This really is what Revelation 19:10 speaks of when it says that "the testimony of Jesus is the spirit of prophecy." What Jesus does for one is prophetic of what He will do for another, and that is what causes people's faith to rise when they hear testimonies.

It is also the reason why, if a person sees the Lord do a specific thing for her in her life, she can pray with strong faith that God will do it for someone else with the same problem. It's like this: any time we have seen God help us overcome in a certain area, we become empowered in that area. For this reason, after I see the Lord heal or help a person with some certain difficulty, I will begin to call others forward who are struggling with the same issue so that the first person who was helped can pray for them as her faith is usually skyrocketing at that point. I can't even begin to remember how many times we have seen the Lord do awesome miracles when we do that in a meeting, but here are just a few that prove the point.

One night while ministering in Michigan, I prayed for a woman who looked to be about thirty years old. She had been born with crooked ankles and no arches in her feet. As I prayed, I could feel her ankles instantly shifting and straightening under my hands, and after about ten minutes she also had perfect arches in her feet. I asked if there was anyone else in attendance that had crooked ankles or flat feet, and a woman came forward who had no arches. The first woman then prayed for her, and after about ten minutes the second woman also received perfect arches in her feet.

Two nights later I was ministering at a church in Canada. I told the audience what we had seen happen a few days earlier in Michigan. I then asked if there was anyone with crooked ankles in the house, and a mother brought her ten-year-old son forward who had also been born with crooked ankles and no arches. I knelt down in front of him and began to pray, but before I could even touch his obviously crooked ankles, they snapped straight and he was instantly healed!

His mother began to scream hysterically when she saw it, and people had to actually take her off to the side to get her calmed down. It turned out she had just decided to accept Jesus into her heart two weeks earlier, and this was only the second time she had ever been in a church and it was really rocking her world.

I then called out if there was anyone else with crooked ankles or flat feet. Another young woman came forward, and I had this ten-year-old boy who had just gotten healed pray for her. After he prayed for her, she got up and unexpectedly ran out of the church to everyone's surprise. Minutes later she returned holding up a large piece of orange construction paper and was showing it to everyone. When she made her way through the crowd to me and I got to see it, I had to laugh. She had gone outside and walked around in the snow with just her socks on and when she came back in she found this piece of paper and stood on it to see what kind of print her feet now made. To her joy there was just her heel and the front of her foot perfectly imprinted on the paper, showing that her feet were no longer flat anymore!

From crooked bones growing straight to bad backs getting healed to addictions and depression getting chased away, we have seen it happen as the healed and delivered pray for others. This is faith in operation! Please remember that the people doing the praying at this point are just normal people out of the crowd and are not church workers. This really is God's ultimate plan and grand design of the way the church should be operating.

It has to be what Jesus meant in John 14:12 when He said, "I tell you the truth, anyone who has faith in me will do what I have been doing. He will do even greater things than these, because I am going to the Father." In case you missed that, let me repeat it. Jesus said that anyone who has faith in Him will do what He did and even greater things! Is that awesome or what? The real question is, do you believe it?

The Importance of Faith

When we study the ministry of Jesus, we find there are about thirty-five different specific miracles that were recorded, but the apostle John who was with Him says that He did many other things that aren't even written down (John 21:24–25). Of those thirty-five miracles there are about eighteen times when He prayed for a certain person or persons to be healed, not counting the people that He brought back from the dead or were healed in large crowds. Six of those eighteen times He directly attributes the person's faith as the reason why they were healed. So for a third of the people who were healed, Jesus specifically said it was their faith that had healed them.

This tells us that for many people God expects them to have faith in order to get their prayers answered. In fact, the Bible says something rather interesting about the time when Jesus was trying to minister in His hometown in Mark 6:5–6. It says, "He could not do any miracles there, except lay his hands on a few sick people and heal them. And he was amazed at their lack of faith." Does it surprise you that the Bible says Jesus *could not* do any miracles there? It used to surprise me until the Lord explained it to me in a way I could understand. This was the analogy He gave me.

Let's say a person you didn't know walked up to you on the street and told you he was going to give you a million dollars and then wrote out a check for one million dollars and held it out to you. (Let's also say for the illustration the check was good.) How many people would actually take the check or much less try to deposit it in their checking account?

Or let's say someone you did know did this to you, but you thought you knew the person well enough to know that the check was worthless because she didn't have the money. She could try as hard as she wanted to bless you, but if you wouldn't take the check, she couldn't give you the money.

This was the way it was for Jesus in His hometown. Because He had grown up there, the people thought they knew Him. When He claimed to be the Christ, they just couldn't believe it and refused to take from Him what was available. The check was there and it was good, but they just wouldn't take it to the bank.

Our faith in God is like the hand that reaches out to take hold of the check. If that hand doesn't go forth, we can't connect to the healings, love, power, forgiveness, mercy, and other blessings that are there waiting for us, so faith is very important—and we need to figure out how to get it.

The Bible says in Romans 10:17, "So faith comes by hearing, and hearing by the word of God" (NKJV). In the context of the chapter this is referring to hearing the message of salvation preached, but many believe it also means listening to any biblical preaching.

In Luke 17 the disciples asked Jesus, "Increase our faith," and He told them if they had the faith of a mustard seed they could tell a tree to be uprooted and planted in the sea and it would obey them. A mustard seed is tiny, so obviously Jesus was telling them that it didn't take much faith to get the job done.

Once the Lord gave me a very simple dream that showed me this exact thing. In this dream I was alone in the living room of a big house, and all of a sudden a lion walked into the room and began to walk back and forth in front of me in a very threatening way. I realized I couldn't run from it, so I just froze with my back against the wall. More lions began to come into the room, and I knew they were about to attack me. Finally one came running from across the room and jumped through the air to pounce on me. I noticed there was a simple window screen leaning against the wall next to me, and I held it up for protection, like a shield. To my amazement the huge lion bounced off of this flimsy little screen like it was a trampoline. Over and over the lions took turns trying to pounce on me, but each time they would bounce off of this feeble little screen that began to bend but never broke.

In Ephesians 6 we are told to take up the shield of faith to extinguish the darts of the evil one. God was showing me at that time in my life my shield of faith was flimsy and so thin I could see through it, but it was still enough to protect me from the enemy!

Doubt Is Destroyed

Doubt, sometimes described as unbelief, is the fifth and last tactic of the enemy that we will discuss, and it is the exact opposite of faith. All the way back to the Garden of Eden the enemy has been planting the seeds of doubt in order to try and trip up humankind, and it has been a scheme that has garnered him some success, so we can see why the Lord would give us the supernatural weapon of faith in order to destroy doubt.

The Bible talks about the affects of doubt when a person prays or asks the Lord for something in James 1:6–7: "But let him ask in faith, with no doubting, for he who doubts is like a wave of the sea driven and tossed by the wind. For let not that man suppose that he will receive anything from the Lord" (NKJV).

One time Jesus's disciples asked Him why they weren't able to cast a demon out of a boy, and His reply matched right up with the last passages from James. He said in Matthew 17:20, "Because of your unbelief; for assuredly, I say to you, if you have faith as a mustard seed, you will say to this mountain, 'Move from here to there,' and it will move; and nothing will be impossible for you" (NKJV).

So just like the spot we read in Luke 17, Jesus lets His disciples know that faith is not the whole issue, as even their tiny little mustard seed of faith had the ability to throw mountains and trees into the sea. He clearly says the problem is their unbelief, their doubt.

Let me share a testimony with you that proves this point.

I was invited to speak at a church I had never been to before but was told by the pastor my testimony would be a stretch for them as they were not used to seeing healings or the Lord move in miracles or that sort of thing. During the praise and worship time the Lord gave me a word of knowledge that someone was dealing with excruciating pain in their right ankle. Up until this point in the ministry

I had never delivered a word of knowledge until the preaching was done and it was time to pray for the people. It was clear the Lord wanted me to do it now, so when I was invited to the podium, I asked who it was who had the horrible pain in their right ankle.

A woman near the front immediately stood up and hobbled to the aisle and said it was her. She said it was so bad she couldn't put weight on it and was even thinking about not staying for the service. I told her that the Lord wanted to heal her and just held out my hand toward her and prayed for her from the podium. I asked how it felt now, and she said that the pain was completely gone in her ankle but that her back still hurt!

I was caught off guard by this response but decided to just pray for her back quickly so I could begin to preach. I prayed from the podium as I did the first time and asked her how her back felt now, and she loudly yelled out, "No change." As she was so close, I decided to just get down from the platform and go lay hands on her when I prayed this time. After doing so, I asked how her back felt now. Again she loudly yelled out, "No change." The cycle repeated itself one more time, and I could tell that the church members were beginning to become uncomfortable and that for whatever reason this woman's back wasn't going to get healed right then. In desperation I prayed one more time, but this time I asked the Lord to just knock her out so we could move on. The power of God hit the woman and she fell to the floor, "slain in the Spirit" as they say. I went back to the podium and began to preach, and the woman didn't wake up or move for at least twenty minutes. When she did, she quietly went back to her seat.

I later ended up talking with the woman at length and found out that her back had been operated on several times and that she had prayed for God to heal it several times. When it wasn't healed, she doubted if it really was His will to heal her back.

God's Will

Over the next few days I spent time in prayer about this woman and her situation as it puzzled me why her ankle was healed but her back wasn't. The Lord then began to reveal some things to me. First, when He gave me the word of knowledge for her ankle, it caused her faith to rise to the point that she easily received her healing. So at that point we know that she had at least a mustard seed of faith in God and that the healing power of God was there to heal. But because of her unanswered prayers for her back in the past, she doubted or had unbelief that God was willing to heal that, so she couldn't receive it. The check was there and it was good, but she just couldn't bring herself to take it to the bank and deposit it.

Any time you or I are praying for anything, we need to have it settled in our mind what God's will is on the subject in general before we can pray and not have doubt or unbelief hindering our prayers. Unfortunately there has been a lot of bad teaching and faulty theology out there throughout the years that the enemy has used to plant seeds of doubt and trip people up.

For instance, let's look at the subject of healing, as in our example of the woman. I don't claim to be an expert on the Bible, but I have read it several times, and you can't show me one single time where Jesus ever turned down a person who came to Him for healing or ever said it wasn't God's will to heal people. In fact, He said just the opposite. He also said that He only did what He saw the Father doing and only said what He heard the Father saying (John 5:19; 12:49–50). If you need some kind of healing in your body, you need to get that question settled in your head and heart first before you pray. Then release it to God, trusting in His method and timetable.

If you have some other type of need, the same thing goes. Just listen to what the second verse from 3 John says about God blessing every part of your life: "Beloved, I pray that you may prosper in *all things* and be in health, just as your soul prospers" (NKJV, emphasis added). Whatever your need is, find places in the Bible that talk about it and then stand on those promises so your faith will grow and your doubt will be destroyed!

I know sometimes it's not as easy as it sounds, but God never said life was going to be easy. He said in this world we would have trouble and tribulations, but that we could take heart because He has overcome the world and destroyed the work of the devil (John 16:33; 1 John 3:8)! But we must also remember that we are told in 1 Peter 5:9 that *we need to actively resist* the devil. We are on the winning team, but we still need to fight!

You read in chapter 5 how I struggled for years with doubt when it came to our finances. It took much time and the complete tearing down of the things I depended on for security before I got to a place of knowing that I really could count on the Lord to financially provide for our family. His promises from the Bible about taking care of our needs and even blessing us were planted in my mind, but my doubt kept those seeds from getting down deep in my heart, so they were dormant for years and the enemy was able to attack.

It doesn't have to be that way for you. Whatever your need is, find promises in the Bible that talk about it and choose this day to believe God's promises more than your circumstances. Let your faith soar so that any doubt is destroyed and those promises can germinate in your heart. I can't tell you how many times I have had the pleasure of praying for people who have already decided and believed in their mind and heart that when they get prayer, God is going to take care of their problem, and when we pray for them, He does. The funny thing is I know my prayer had nothing to do with them getting what they needed in those cases; it was them using the mighty weapon of faith, and my prayer was just a point of contact!

Part Three
The Five Giants We All Face in Life

Part Three

The Five Giants We All Face in Life

I N THE INTRODUCTION to part 2 of the book I explained to you how on April 22, 2010, two friends of mine walked up to me at church and gave me similar words from the Lord within minutes of each other. The first man, Earl, said all he was given was the number five, and the second man, Todd, said it was the number five found in the account of David and Goliath and from the life of David. The Lord told him he was to remind me that David picked up five stones from the brook when he faced Goliath and that he and his men faced five giants during his lifetime. Todd went on to say the Lord said this number five represented some very important truths and if I would seek Him on these truths, He would reveal them to me.

While I was praying and fasting over the following days the Lord revealed to me what the five stones represented as well as what the five giants represented and how this was to be the outline for the book you are now reading.

In part 2 you read how David's five stones were prophetic of the complete arsenal of weapons the Lord has for believers and what each one of those main weapons are. Now in part 3 we will discuss the significance of David facing a total of five giants during his life and what that means for us.

David's Five Giants

After we read the account of David fighting Goliath in 1 Samuel 17, we later read in 2 Samuel 21 that he and his men ended up facing four more giants, for a total of five giants. As I began to research all the places I found the number five used in the Bible, I found a shocking pattern of God's people having to fight against five enemies. Starting clear back with Moses in Numbers 31, we see that he had to fight against the five kings of Midian. Then in Joshua 10 we read that Joshua had to fight against the five Amorite kings. Finally in David's time we see the biggest enemy the Israelites had were the Philistines, and, you guessed it, they too had five rulers who were set up in a confederacy of five principle cities.

Now please bear with me as we take the time to lay this out and make sense of it.

Upon looking up the history of these five cities, I found some very interesting verses from the Book of Joshua about them. After Joshua died, there still were unconquered parts of the Promised Land the Israelites needed to fight for, as not all of the enemy nations had been driven out yet, and these five Philistine cities were some of those lands. We read in Judges 3:1–4 why that was: "These are the nations the LORD left to test all those Israelites who had not experienced any of the wars of Canaan (he did this only to teach warfare to the descendants of the Israelites who had not had previous battle experience): the five rulers of the Philistines, all the Canaanites.... They were left to test the Israelites to see whether they would obey the LORD's commands, which he had given their forefathers through Moses."

So God left these enemy nations in the lives of His people to test them, teach them warfare through battle experience, and see if they would obey His commands.

When I looked up these five Philistine cities on a map, I found that they were arranged in basically a semicircle around Bethlehem, which was where David was from. But there was one of the Philistine cities that was definitely closer than the others—the city of Gath. It was only about twenty miles from Bethlehem, so it was right in David's backyard. It is important to note the Bible clearly tells us that all five of the giants David faced were descendants of the same man who, interestingly enough, came from this city of Gath.

When I looked up the word *Gath* in Strong's concordance, I found that it meant "winepress." When I did some research on what a winepress was, I found it to be a device that is used to exert controlled pressure on grapes in order to free the valuable juice from the fruit. I also found that the pressure must be carefully controlled in order to avoid crushing the seeds and releasing a great deal of undesirable contaminants into the juice and thereby causing it to become bitter and ruining it.

The Lord finally led me to one last thing that ties this all together. Several times already I have quoted Jesus from John 16:33 where He says, "In the world you will have tribulation; but be of good cheer, I have overcome the world" (NKJV). When we look up the word *tribulation* from that passage and others, we can see how this all fits together. According to Strong's concordance, the Greek word for "tribulation" means "pressure, oppression, stress, anguish, adversity, affliction, crushing, squashing, squeezing, and distress." It describes suffering caused by an internal or external pressure. But most telling of all for our example, it also describes crushing grapes in a winepress!

The Five Giants We All Face in Life

Just as the five stones were prophetic of the five weapons God gives us, the five giants David faced are prophetic of the five different giants we all must face in this life.

The Lord showed me that each person who lives in this world actually only has five areas of problems:

1. Relational

2. Spiritual

3. Physical

4. Emotional

5. Financial

In fact, there isn't a problem we can encounter that isn't contained in one of these five categories. He also showed me that each one of the five main miracles that have happened in my life correspond to each one of these areas, just as each one of those miracles involved one of the supernatural weapons He gives.

The five Philistine cities were located in a semicircle around David, enabling each one to come at him from a different direction. This too is prophetic as the five giants we face in our life are able to come at us from different directions as well, due to the broad range of matter they cover.

The fact that all five of the giants David faced descended from Gath, an area very close to his home, and that Gath means winepress—a tool that exerts controlled pressure in order to yield something valuable—is also prophetic. The giants we face in our lives, the ones that come from our backyard, also put pressure on us and squeeze us. Just as Jesus said, we will go through tribulation. We learned that is just what tribulation describes—suffering caused from an internal or external pressure, and again, the description even compares it to crushing grapes in a winepress. So the giants we face in our lives can and will at times cause us tribulation or trouble.

The good news is that when the process is done, it can yield something valuable! What determines if that happens or not is our attitude and perspective on the situation.

We learned from the passages in Judges that God allowed the enemy nations to remain in the lives of His people in order to test them, teach them warfare through battle experience, and see if they would obey His commands. We need to remember that He can use the trials we go through to do the same thing today.

God is not the author of our trials, but they will come along. When they do, it gives us the opportunity to exercise our faith and obedience to Him. Hebrews 5:8 says of Jesus, "Although he was a son, he learned obedience from what he suffered." We also need to remember that the Bible tells us in 1 Peter 5:9–10, "You know that your brothers throughout the world are undergoing the same kind of sufferings. And the God of all grace, who called you to his eternal glory in Christ, after you have suffered a little while, will himself restore you and make you strong, firm, and steadfast."

Just as the winepress operator is careful not to allow too much pressure to be exerted on the grapes so that the valuable juice is not made bitter, so our loving Father doesn't want us to come under so much pressure that we become bitter or ruined. We are to retain a right attitude and continue to be obedient and hopeful despite the hardships and giants we face, knowing that victory can only come after a battle and trusting that God will empower us to overcome. As 1 Corinthians 15:57 says, "But thanks be to God, who gives us the victory through our Lord Jesus Christ" (NKJV).

Over the next five chapters we will take a more in-depth look at each of the giants we face in this life through various real-life testimonies that show what victory looks like in those areas.

Chapter 11

Relational Problems

Relationships Restored!

O NE NIGHT WHILE I was preaching at a church, I noticed a young woman in her early twenties who was obviously struggling with God during my talk. At the end of the service I invited people to the front for prayer, and her mother brought her forward. I asked what her prayer request was, and she said she had severe pain in her stomach for the last several years that never went away. She had been to many doctors who had done many tests, tried various medicines, and even did two different exploratory surgeries trying to find the cause of her pain, but they never could find out what it was.

As I began to pray for her, the Lord gave me a word of knowledge that she had strong unforgiveness for her father. I stopped praying and told her what I believed the Lord had said and asked her if that was true. When I did, her eyes got very big and she looked at her mom in astonishment before breaking down in tears. She ended up nodding her head yes that she did. I talked with her a bit about what it looks like to forgive someone and how it is an intentional choice we make more than it is a feeling we have. I also explained that even if the person doesn't deserve to be forgiven in our eyes because what they did hurt us badly, God still tells us to forgive anyway.

I ended up leading her through a short prayer of forgiveness for her dad. I prayed for her healing again, commanding the pain to go in the name of Jesus. When we finished, she was completely pain free for the first time in years. She said she felt very light and also felt a heat and tingling in her body.

The next day her mom came back and told me the rest of the story. The mother had been a lifelong drug user but just recently came to the Lord and had brought her adult daughter, who didn't believe in God or go to church, to get prayer for her stomach. During my testimony the young woman began to question if God possibly was real and told the Lord that if He was real, she wanted to have some kind of personal experience with Him, like the things I was talking about. Then when they came forward for prayer and the Lord gave a word of knowledge about something I couldn't have known about and she ended up getting totally healed and feeling His presence physically in her body, faith rose up in her, and she knew it was God answering her prayer and decided to accept Him into her heart right then.

She then went home and called her father and told him she forgave him for everything he had done to her and wanted to start the process of restoring their relationship. Her mom said that at about 2:00 a.m. her daughter had then called her and asked if she could get a Bible from her as she had lots of questions about God.

Relational Giants

We all have various relationships with other people that can vary in depth and meaning, but at any given time one of these connections can blow up and turn into a giant of a problem in our lives. Obviously the more important the relationship is to us, the more it can affect us, but even peripheral relationships have the ability to cause great havoc in our lives. Maybe it is that "jerk at work" who gets under your skin or the "naughty neighbor" who throws his dog poop in your yard.

As long as we are alive in this world we are going to have to deal with people, and because people are born with a sinful nature and therefore are not always perfect, there are going to be problems in our relationships. When these problems arise, it is the choice of the individual as to how they are going to respond to them, and whatever choice the individual makes will determine what impact or affect it has on his or her life. The only choice we can make that will bless us is to forgive those who hurt us. All other choices will only bring grief in the end.

For example, bitterness and hatred if left in the heart will end up growing like cancer and eventually consume the person holding on to them. In much the same way the person who tries to just ignore the seeds of conflict planted in him from a past or even current troubled relationship will find those hidden seeds coming to fruition eventually. Quite commonly that fruit will show up in a completely different area of their life—from anger issues to addictions to health issues, the list goes on and on.

Unforgiveness Kills

Just like the young woman in the first example, it is quite common for a person's health to suffer. The pain in her stomach was a direct result of unforgiveness for her dad. I can't even begin to remember how many times I have prayed for a health issue to be healed in someone, and the Lord will then give me a word for them about unforgiveness in their heart that needs to be dealt with first.

Once while I was ministering at a woman's conference, a lady came forward for prayer with literally a list of physical issues written down on a piece of paper. I prayed for her for several minutes with absolutely no change in anything. When I asked the Lord what was going on, He told me that she had unforgiveness for her ex-husband, her brother, and another person from her childhood.

I stopped praying and asked her if that was true, and she admitted it was. I explained to her that unforgiveness is a sin and what Ephesians 4:26–27 said about not even going to bed angry so that we don't give the devil a "foothold" or "place" in our life. When we do, he then has legal ground to attack us, and that includes our health. She heard what I was saying but said she couldn't forgive the people because they didn't deserve it. I explained that we don't deserve to be forgiven either, but God still forgives us.

I told her to stand off to the side by herself and spend some time praying about it, and I encouraged her to choose to forgive her ex-husband and the other two from her heart. I would then pray over her again if she wanted.

When she came back to me an hour later, I went to pray for her, and before my hands could touch her, the power of God touched her and she dropped to the floor. Lights out. When she came to some time later, she was amazed to find all of the various pains and issues in her body healed.

The first time I prayed there was no change, and the second time I prayed she got gloriously healed. The only difference was her admitting her sin and then forgiving those who had hurt her. She had been fighting with a relational giant and didn't realize it had attacked her health! James 5:16 says, "Therefore confess your sins to each other and pray for each other that you may be healed."

One night at a church a man came forward. When I asked what his prayer request was, he hesitated before saying he was "too young to feel as old as he did." He then went on to tell me a whole pile of things that were wrong in his body. As I began to pray, the Lord told me this was because unrepentant sin had opened a door for him to be attacked by the enemy.

I told him what I felt the Lord had said, and he adamantly denied it. So I prayed again and asked the Lord to reveal the sin. The Holy Spirit said that this was a relationship issue and he had not only wronged someone but also was bitter toward the person after he did it and he knew exactly whom he did it to.

The man instantly hung his head and began to sob. He walked away from me and knelt down in front of the pastor of the church, grabbed him by the feet, and asked for forgiveness. The pastor stood the man up, and they talked at length before the man left.

Later the pastor told me the rest of the story. Apparently one morning during a church service with hundreds of people present the pastor said something the man didn't doctrinally agree with, and he stood up in the service and began to argue with the pastor. It got so bad the pastor ended up sitting down and not even finishing his sermon. This had happened about a year before, and this was actually the first time the man had been back. Then he only came because he wanted to hear my testimony at a special service they held.

The lesson we learn is that because of a relational giant that caused him to sin and not repent, the Lord said he had opened himself up to an attack of the enemy that had caused his sicknesses. There is also the issue of "coming against the Lord's anointed." I'm sure there are many pastors who would love me to preach that sermon at their church!

Another time a woman called me on the phone for prayer for a physical problem. When I asked her what the problem was, she said if I was really a man of God, I should be able to tell her. As we prayed, the Lord told me that her biggest problem was unforgiveness and then said that in addition to her health problem, she was also dealing with financial issues. Then the Lord showed me a vision of a pair of very skinny legs growing thicker and had me quote Isaiah 40:31: "Those who hope in the LORD will renew their strength. They will soar on wings like eagles; they will run and not grow weary, they will walk and not be faint." The more I spoke, the harder the woman began to cry until she was sobbing.

After she composed herself, she told me that she had been a nurse and was having a physical issue. She went to a doctor who performed some type of test on her, and her body had a bad reaction to the chemicals. It ended up almost crippling her. She could no longer work, which caused great financial burden on her, and she was barely able to walk as the muscles in her legs and the rest of her body had begun to waste away. This was hard for her because she used to be an avid runner and very active. Because of all this she had grown to hate the doctor who had given her that unneeded test and just couldn't seem to forgive him.

I bring this story up because although this woman had some very serious things going on in her life, the Lord said her biggest problem was unforgiveness! He then proved it was Him talking by giving the vision that showed what the problem was. She was fighting a relational giant and it was winning, but God was ready to intervene so she could get better in more ways than one. The part that brought her the most comfort was that in the vision the Lord gave me her legs were getting bigger. The Lord said she would walk and not grow faint and even run and not grow weary!

Only God Can Fill in the Holes

A mountain of a man came forward for prayer one night for his addiction to cigarettes. As I prayed for him, the Lord told me that one of his parents never loved him or showed him any love. So I asked him which one of his parents didn't love him. When I did, he clenched his fists and answered me through gritted teeth, "My mother!"

I had no idea why the Lord brought that up until He gave me the next bit of information. The Holy Spirit said that because the man never had a relationship with his mother, it caused a hole in his heart. As soon as he allowed the Lord to come into that void and fill it up, he would no longer be addicted to cigarettes. When I spoke it out, the man broke down weeping as God began to minister to his heart.

This man had been fighting a relational giant his whole life and never even realized it. Not getting the love he needed from his mother was the root cause of his addiction to cigarettes. Without God intervening, neither one of us would have known it. That's what God wants to do in our lives; He wants to get down to the root issues so our hearts can be healed and so relationships can be mended.

One day a woman called our ministry number to order some books. I answered and took her order. She was being very gruff and kind of nasty on the phone. After taking her order, I told her whom she had on the line. She was embarrassed and tried to get off the phone quickly, but the Lord told me I was to pray for her first.

As soon as I began to pray, the Lord told me this woman had someone in her life named Ruth and the Lord wanted her to minister to Ruth out of His love in order to draw her into a saving relationship with Him. When I asked her who Ruth was, she said it was her sister-in-law and that she wasn't a believer. She went on to say that if she was to minister to her in love, it would have to be in God's love because she hated her!

I appreciated her honesty and the fact that God was going right to the root issue and addressing her lack of love while encouraging her that He could fill her with His love for her sister-in-law. I also thought it was significant that the Lord wanted to mend this relationship so the other woman could be brought into a saving faith with Him. What enemies do you have whom God wants you to reach for Him? God's desire is to restore relationships, and His reasons why are often far above what we could imagine.

I previously mentioned a friend of mine from church named Earl. He was one of the two guys who got a word from the Lord for me of the significance of the number five for this book. He has a great testimony about relational giants and the restoring nature of God. Early in life he married a woman named Denise. After three years they ended up getting a divorce. He struggled with alcohol use and wasn't an active believer for many years, but God chased him down, and he ended up getting set free from alcohol and back into church because of some serious prayer. After thirteen years he and Denise ended up remarrying and now are both actively involved in ministry at their local church!

This is the kind of God we serve, one who gives us every weapon we need in order to fight the battles that we face in this life. In chapter 1 you read how I had been repeatedly molested as a child. This was a relational giant that caused me much grief, but God used the mighty weapon of the Word through that Sunday school teacher so I would know who Jesus was and call out to Him.

If you are dealing with some relational problems in your life that have turned into giants, or if you have some old battle wounds from the past, then know this: God is rooting for you and wants to see you be made whole and have peace in your heart. He wants you to be able to live a life of victory over any giants you are facing. Second Corinthians 2:14 says, "Thanks be to God who always leads us in triumph in Christ" (NKJV).

Chapter 12

Spiritual Problems

Victory Through Jesus!

A FEW DAYS BEFORE I was to leave for a crusade in Honduras, one of the people who prays for our ministry called to say that the Lord had given her the same vision over and over about our upcoming trip. In the vision she was lying in a bed and opening her eyes from a coma or unnaturally deep sleep of some kind. As her eyes would begin to open, she would see me standing there. I was shining, and light was coming from around me. When she asked the Lord what it meant, He told her that "many eyes will be opened."

On the way to the crusade grounds that first night the Lord reminded me of a dream He had given me a long time before. I was in a building that I knew was in a third-world nation, and I was praying for a woman who was blind in a way, as she could only see in black and white, with no color. After prayer her eyes were healed, but I knew this was somehow symbolic. I mentioned it to the people in the car and said that as soon as I saw the inside, I would be able to tell if it was the building or not because I remembered the way it looked behind the woman as I prayed for her in my dream.

Once we got inside, I knew immediately that it was the same building. After preaching that night I shared my dream with the people and invited any women who had any type of eye problems or blindness to come forward. Fifteen women came to the front and gathered in a semicircle on the right side of the platform. When I stood in front of them, I saw the woman from my dream right in the middle with seven women on each side of her, and I realized she was in the exact place in the building she had been in my dream.

We prayed for each woman. When we were finished, fourteen out of the fifteen claimed they were healed. We saw two or three eyes that were cloudy white or discolored clear up perfectly as well as some very red eyes get clear and so on. Some of the women had been blind in one eye or another. Some just had very poor vision in one or both eyes. To this day I still have not seen so many people with blindness get healed at one time. Over the next few days we saw a few more people get their eyes healed. On the last day of the crusade a man born blind got about 50 percent of his vision and could see somewhat after prayer.

This really excited me. I began to pray about it and ask the Lord what was going on. The answer I got surprised me. The Lord told me that many of the people in the area were spiritually blind, and He was opening people's eyes in the natural to show what was happening in the spirit realm. Their spiritual eyes were being opened! He was using the TV shows, the crusade, and the rest of the ministry work He had us doing while there in order to push back the darkness and shine His light so many people's spiritual eyes would be opened.

When I got home and reread the vision our prayer warrior had about her heavy eyes opening, the Lord telling her that "many eyes will be opened," and even the fact that she saw the light shining, it confirmed what I felt the Lord had told me. I also looked up the dream I had in my journal and found the Lord had given it to me exactly one year, one month, and one day before it happened, just so there couldn't be any mistaking it was a "God thing." Even the fact that in my journal I wrote that the Holy Spirit put on my heart that her "seeing in color was important" showed the value God sees in our spiritual eyes being opened.

Spiritual Giants

One of the five giants we face in this life is spiritual. Because we can't see them, spiritual giants are usually the hardest to discern. For this reason they very well might be the most dangerous to us. We are in a spiritual war and the foes we face are playing for keeps. Jesus tells us in John 10:10 that our enemy comes *only* to steal, kill, and destroy. The devil and his cohorts want to see people be condemned to hell, and if someone is a believer, they want to keep them beat down to the point that they are useless for the kingdom. That is the bad news.

The good news is that according to Luke 10:19 Jesus has given us authority over them. We are able to "overcome all the power of the enemy." First John 4:4 says that the One who is in us is stronger/greater than our enemies in this world. If that weren't enough to make us feel secure, we have already seen from the Bible where the Lord has issued us an assortment of supernatural weapons that have the ability to beat our enemy every time if used correctly.

In Ephesians 6:11–12 we read, "Put on the full armor of God so that you can take your stand against the devil's schemes. For our struggle is not against flesh and blood, but against the rulers, against the authorities, against the powers of this dark world and against the spiritual forces of evil in the heavenly realms." So we have this long list of our enemies given in a way that shows they have an order to them, a hierarchy. We are told to put on the armor of God so we can stand against their "schemes." The following verses go on to describe the various pieces of armor. In verse 16 it says, "Above all, taking the shield of faith with which you will be able to quench all the fiery darts of the wicked one" (NKJV).

Our Enemy Has Been Disarmed

In Colossians 2:15 we read that Jesus disarmed our enemy. In these verses from Ephesians we read that he only has "schemes." Second Corinthians 2:11 says, "We are not unaware of his schemes." So not only does the Lord take his weapons away and leave him with just schemes, but also He then tells us what those schemes are through the Bible!

It is important to note that in Ephesians 6:16 it tells us to *above all* take up the shield of faith in order to quench the fiery darts of the enemy. If you were in a battle from that time, wouldn't you rather want to throw a spear, a javelin, or even rocks from a catapult rather than darts that are disintegrating because they are burning up? Yes, you would, but our enemy can't because he has been disarmed. That is why he can only throw flaming darts that have the appearance of being more deadly than they really are, which is one of his schemes. He tries to use lies or fear to appear more powerful than he is, much like the petty criminal who pretends to have a gun in his pocket while trying to rob someone. If the person getting robbed is too afraid to call his bluff, the thief gets away with the robbery. The Lord tells us take up the shield of faith as we are not unaware of these schemes! Call the enemy's bluff!

The Lord gave me two different dreams two years apart that show this exact thing. In one dream I was with a group of people, and we were being chased and attacked by a wolf. It was very scary sounding, and at first we were afraid. Then I realized it was half dead as its hindquarters were wasting away and its lower jaw was missing! I ended up fighting it off quite easily as it really couldn't bite without its lower jaw and with weak muscles. It was aggressive and it was persistent, but since it didn't have any way to really harm me, I could chase it away, but it would try to come back after a bit.

In the second dream I was again with a group of people. This time we were looking at a dismembered alligator. All of a sudden the individual parts loosely came back together and began to chase us around. We were scared even though we could see that the lower half of its jaw was missing. And because it was dismembered, it had no strength. When I awoke, the Lord told me that His people are scared of things that are harmless as they have been beaten, dismembered, and have no power left in them.

Then my daily devotional that morning talked about the same thing. It said the temptation is to focus on the problem. That's what the devil planned on and that is why he sent it in the first place: to draw your attention away from God. Don't fall for this tactic or scheme. Focus your thoughts on God. As you do, the force of faith will flow out of you and repel every form of darkness! Our enemy might be persistent, but he is already beaten.

Focus on God, Not the Problem

One morning before I was to minister at a church, the Lord gave me a dream. In the dream the Holy Spirit was standing next to me and a blonde woman with shoulder-length hair was standing about ten feet away looking the other way. The Holy Spirit told me she was to be called Jennifer, so I called out "Jennifer" several times, but she never turned her head or looked. The Holy Spirit then said she had never been called that name before. We were then standing next to her, and she had her head bent down as if there were heavy weights tied to it. She said that her head was so heavy she just couldn't hold it anymore and maybe somebody else should because she was about to give up. Then the Holy Spirit touched her, and I watched as a demon I hadn't seen was thrown off of her back.

That day after preaching I told the people I believed there was somebody in attendance who had been named Jennifer but had never been called it a day in her life, or more likely there was somebody there who was supposed to have been named Jennifer but wasn't. A woman stood up in the back, and I immediately knew it was her when I saw her shoulder length-blonde hair, so I invited her forward.

She stood in front of me and the two pastors from the church stood behind her. The Holy Spirit told me to tell her to put out her hands in front of her, palms up. I then said that the Lord said she was carrying a very heavy weight, a burden that she was not designed or supposed to be carrying. When I spoke it out, she began to fall forward as if there were one thousand pounds of weight in her hands. The two pastors had to literally grab her shoulders to hold her from falling forward.

Then the Lord told me to tell her He knew the number of hairs on her head and He knew about this situation, this burden she was carrying, and she was supposed to release it to Him. So I told her to now turn her hands over, symbolically letting this burden go. When she did, she sprang backward, and the pastors had to hold her to keep her from falling down backward. The Lord then told me to tell her not give up, but that she should just focus on Him and trust Him.

At lunch the pastor told me that earlier just that week he had a meeting with her and her husband, and he had told her the exact same thing, but she just didn't receive it. She had three adult children who each had some very serious problems, and she had become consumed by it to the point of almost spinning out of control herself. She worked in ministry and was even talking about quitting her job because she was so beside herself with grief and worry.

A few days later I had the opportunity to speak with the woman. She told me it felt like a heavy weight had been taken off her back and she was now back to her old self, happy and full of peace. I asked what the deal was with her name. She said her mother had her at a very young age and her grandmother had chosen the name Jennifer for her, but after her mom was in labor for nineteen hours, she decided she should be able to name her own baby and called her another name instead. She said at this point anybody who even knew that had already died, so when I called it out, she knew it had to be the Lord speaking.

I bring this up because the dream the Lord gave me showed that it was actually a demon that was "on her back" oppressing her. Her deep grief was caused by this spiritual giant who used the worry she was experiencing to get her to focus on the problem and take her focus off of God. This then gave the enemy an open door to allow himself to attach to her and oppress her.

Victory Through Jesus

Over the years we have seen many examples of spiritual giants causing problems in people's lives, from full-out demonic possession to the customary demonic oppression. It is out there. If the problem persists, there is almost always a definable reason that can be found that somehow has given the enemy legal ground to do what he is doing.

One night while I was ministering in Central America, right in the middle of my message, the Lord opened my spiritual eyes. I saw there was a demon inside a ten-year-old little boy sitting near the middle of the church. I stopped preaching and had the interpreter call the mom forward with the boy and ask her about the child. She said that he had turned into a naughty boy and that sometimes he would wake up in the middle of the night and start speaking in a language they couldn't understand and had even chased them around with a knife while doing this before. He had also become an epileptic about the same time.

I began to pray over him. As soon as I did, he fell down and began to go into what looked like a grand mal seizure before arching his back and then looking as though he was dead. I then saw one of his eyes just barely crack open as the demon peeked out at me before the eye quickly shut again. I knelt down beside the boy and whispered to the demon that I knew he was still there and he was going to have to go in the name of Jesus. I used the mighty weapon of authority and commanded the demon to go in the name of Jesus. The boy shook violently and then went limp. When he got up off the floor, his face somehow looked different, and he had a whole different countenance about him, much more peaceful.

We asked the mother when these problems had started, and she said it was about the time another family member had moved into their house with them. After asking a few more questions, we found out this other person was also heavily involved with the occult. It became clear the occult practices going on in the house were what opened the door for this child to become possessed.

There are many other spiritual doors we can open without even realizing we are doing it. Many people are aware of the obvious things like drugs, alcohol, occult practices, witchcraft, and the like, but few people know that unforgiveness, defiant unrepentant sin, fear, trauma, and even believing a lie of the enemy—just to name a few—can leave us open to an attack of the enemy.

I want to state here that I have found some groups of people who would try to debunk the idea that evil spirits are active or can do things to influence or even control people, much less Christians. On the other hand I have met people who believe that almost everything that happens is because of some evil spirit. We need to be careful to take a biblically balanced approach to this subject and be honest with ourselves and others. If something is just sin or the normal workings of life, so be it, but if it is demonic in nature, we need to address that also.

In chapter 2 you read how I was addicted to drugs and alcohol for over twenty years and how that missionary woman who didn't know me gave me a word from the Lord that my addiction was really a spiritual problem caused by the demons that had attached to me when I was molested as a child. I was fighting against a spiritual giant all those years and never really knew it. When she and her husband identified it and used the weapon of authority on it, it was over!

It doesn't matter what the enemy might have used to attack you in the past or even in the present; the good news is there is victory over the spiritual giants we face through the name of Jesus! As 1 John 5:5 says, "Who is it that overcomes the world? Only he who believes Jesus is the son of God."

Chapter 13

Physical Problems

Healing Miracles Happen Today!

S ome time ago I was speaking out on the West Coast when we got to see the Lord do quite an astounding miracle.

I had spoken at a fund-raiser on a Saturday night for Worldwide Heart to Heart Ministries, which is a great nonprofit we work with that does a lot in Honduras with orphans and other needy people. Afterward a woman named LeAnne Gunderson came up to me and asked if I would pray for her son. I found out he wasn't there, so I invited the woman to bring him to the church where I would be speaking the next morning.

The next day I gave my testimony and then prayed a group prayer over the entire church before praying for people one on one. LeAnne and her husband, Mike, brought the young man, Christopher, forward for prayer along with his grandma Linda and his brother Ryan. LeAnne and Christopher began to explain how he had been born with a very rare disease with a long name. The disease caused his stomach to be paralyzed and his intestines and GI tract to not work the way they should. When Christopher was a baby, the doctors told LeAnne and Mike their son was likely going to die, and he almost did a few times, but they were always able to resuscitate him.

In order to live at all they installed two tubes in his abdomen:

the G-tube was used to drain out the saliva, mucus, and bile that collected in his paralyzed stomach, and the J-tube was used to feed him liquid food. At the time of prayer he was sixteen years old and had never eaten a single meal in his entire life! Because of this he had low energy, and his physical growth had been slightly stunted along with having to suffer from daily digestive issues, including much stomach pain. Not only that, but he also had to hook up to machines to be fed a few times a day and also drain out his G-tube daily, and sometimes twice daily, as nothing could get through his stomach.

I wanted the whole family to be involved in our prayer, so we gathered in kind of a circle. I had Christopher get in the middle. I started by explaining that I couldn't perform any miracles, but I knew Jesus could, and He gets all the glory and praise as our healer. I also told him I didn't know what the Lord's timetable or method for healing him was, but we would pray that God would do it right now. I then placed my left hand on his right shoulder and began to pray.

I could feel a strong presence of the Lord and knew God was doing something. Christopher began to tremble, and his face started to look a little flushed when all of a sudden he started to hunch forward and said, "Something is wrong. Something is happening to my tube." I asked him if he needed to sit down, and he said, "No." Then the Lord spoke to me and said He wasn't finished yet, and I was to put my hands back on Christopher and keep praying.

As I continued to pray, I could see the end of his top tube beginning to vibrate or pulse through his shirt, and then the vibration looked like it went down his abdomen. Christopher looked overwhelmed, and his mother later said she had never seen that look on his face before.

He said later that when I had prayed over the entire church, a light vibration or pulsing had started in his body, but when I placed my hand on him and began to pray, he felt an electrical shock that went through his body from his right shoulder where my hand was, through his chest, to the top tube. It was at that point that he said something was wrong because the electrical shock was strong enough that it stung. When I continued to pray, he felt the vibration and pulsating caused from the "electrical shock" go through his entire GI system. It was during that time we saw his tubes pulsating. The pulsating vibrations ended up lasting for several minutes.

Later that day he began to complain of a strange pain in his stomach he had never felt before. As he described it, his father said what he was describing was the way he would describe it if he were hungry. That day Christopher ate the first meal he ever had in his life at sixteen years of age, and he did it at a Chinese restaurant! This was no small thing, because if his stomach wouldn't have been healed, he could have gotten very sick from just a few bites and would have had to go get it pumped. When they checked his G-tube later that night and the next morning it was empty, proving his stomach was now working and had been healed!

God not only healed his paralyzed stomach, but his faulty intestines and his whole entire GI track were healed as well. His stomach pains and all digestive issues were gone from that day forward. He has since gotten a clean bill of health from the doctors and had his tubes removed for good. For the first time in his life those tubes are not poking out from under his shirt!

One of the other things God did that day for Christopher had to do with another lifelong problem he dealt with—stuttering. Christopher used to stutter all the time, but since that day he rarely stutters! There is so much more to this story than I have room to talk about here, but you can go to a site his mother started that tells it all: www.christophersmiraclestory.blogspot.com. I think it is also interesting to note that the church where this family regularly attended was not the kind of church that would ever do laying-on-of-hands-type prayer or even embrace that sort of thing. God is still in the miracle business today, healing those who come to Him, regardless of what anybody else's opinion is!

Physical Giants

There are various issues we can have with our physical body, but it is most often some type of infirmity—weakness, sickness, defect, or disease. If a person has never been sick or weak, there is a high probability at some point in his life he will be. Anyone who has ever been seriously ill can tell you that physical giants are real and can be very intimidating and down right terrifying for some. Even short-term illnesses and minor problems can bring great havoc upon our lives and routines.

You read in chapter 3 how badly I was hurt after the truck fell on top of me and how I had to have several operations and stay in the hospital for a long time. This was a physical giant in my life that by the grace of God I came through. Now I am able to even see all the good the Lord has brought out of this tragedy, although I know it wasn't in His perfect will for it to happen and He didn't cause it.

It doesn't take long, after doing a bit of research in the Bible, to find out who the author of these physical giants is. We are told in Genesis 3 and Romans 8 that after sin entered the world because of the devil, the earth came under a curse. Jesus leaves no room for doubt when He shows us in John 10:10 that the devil comes to steal, kill, and destroy. Then there are the various times He reinforces this as He prays for people's healing and makes sure to say who caused the sickness in the first place. An example would be in Luke 13:16 where He is speaking of a crippled woman who was just healed: "Then should not this woman...whom Satan has kept bound for eighteen long years, be set free on the Sabbath day from what bound her?"

The last verse I want to share with you is also very clear who the author of sickness is, but what is exciting about this one is that it also gives us the cure. Acts 10:38 says, "How God anointed Jesus of Nazareth with the Holy Spirit and power, and how He went around doing good and healing all who were under the power of the devil, because God was with Him."

The Holy Spirit Sent to Empower

This verse explains why Jesus never did a miracle until He was baptized, as that is when the Holy Spirit came down on Him. Some believe the miracles He did while here were because He was God, but we read in Philippians 2 He chose to lay down His godhood while on earth, so He needed the Holy Spirit in Him in order to perform miracles while here. If the miracles Jesus did were because He was operating as God, He couldn't have said in John 14:12 we would do the same things He did and even greater things than He did, because we are obviously not God and never have the chance to be.

Jesus was sent to be the perfect example of how man was to live and operate in this life, and that is through the guidance and power of the Holy Spirit living inside of us. That is why He told His followers in John 16:7, "It is to your advantage that I go away; for if I do not go away, the Helper will not come to you; but if I depart, I will send Him to you" (NKJV). Jesus knew in order for us to live victoriously we needed the Helper, the Holy Spirit, so He went away physically so that He could live in each of us spiritually through the indwelling presence of the Holy Spirit. This is really exciting because it is the whole reason we can still expect and see healing miracles happen today—or any other miracles for that matter!

Let me share a quick example of what that looks like. One night while praying for people at a healing service on the East Coast, I prayed for a woman, and after I finished, she walked away. As I began to pray for the next person in line, all of a sudden the Holy Spirit spoke to me and said He wanted me to go find that last woman and pray for her back. I began to scan the crowd and finally spotted the woman about to exit the building, but there were a few hundred people between her and me. Thankfully, just as she got to the door, she turned around and I was able to wave her back to the front.

When she finally got back to me, I told her what the Holy Spirit had said and asked her what was wrong with her back. She said she was born with a birth defect and because of it couldn't bend forward, and she always had pain in her back. We prayed a quick prayer. When the prayer was over, the woman bent forward and almost touched her toes. She said it was the first time in her fifty-one years of life she had been able to bend that far forward, and all the pain in her back was gone.

I can't remember what her prayer request was the first time, but I know it had nothing to do with her back. Although she never mentioned it, the Holy Spirit knew about her birth defect and wanted to heal it for her, so He told me about it and then had me find her so He could take care of it. The great part is this kind of Spirit-led lifestyle is what Jesus wants and makes available for all believers! As He said in John 14:12, "Anyone who has faith in me will do what I have been doing."

God's Will to Heal

There are so many places in the Bible that tell us what God's will is in regard to our physical giants that there shouldn't be a question about this in anyone's mind, unless they don't know about Jesus. I've found several well-meaning, good-hearted people who have unknowingly or even knowingly based their answer to that question on things other than an honest, open-minded study of what the Bible says about healing.

Unfortunately there are those who teach that God no longer does miracles, and it is no longer possible for people to pray for each other and see miracles happen. This teaching or doctrine is then taken at face value by the people in the pews of that church or those attending that Bible school simply because they trust those telling it to them. (Don't try to tell this to Christopher from the beginning of this chapter or to the woman from the last account or to me for that matter, because we are all living proof miracles still do happen when believers pray for each other!)

Then there are those who have prayed for someone to be healed and that person wasn't, or they knew about someone who was prayed for and wasn't healed, or they have prayed for healing for themselves and it never came, so they come to the "logical" conclusion that it must not be God's will to heal sometimes. These people have decided to base their theology on experience, which is a very dangerous thing to do as we should only ever base our theology, doctrine, or belief systems on what the Word of God says—nothing else. If our experiences then line up with the Word of God, then our experiences have only been validated. They do not set the standard.

It is clear we all must die at some point and that we are each given an allotted amount of time to live. That being said, it is also clear that while God never promises we won't get sick, He does give us many promises in the Bible that while we are alive, He is our healer. Second Corinthians 1:20 says, "No matter how many promises God has made, they are 'Yes' in Christ." Here are just a few of those promises:

> I am the LORD, who heals you.
>
> —EXODUS 15:26

> Praise the LORD, O my soul, and forget not all his benefits—who forgives all your sin and heals all your diseases.
>
> —PSALM 103:2–3

> When evening came, many who were demon possessed were brought to him, and he drove out the spirits with a word and healed all the sick. This was to fulfill what was spoken through the prophet Isaiah: "He took up our infirmities and carried our diseases."
>
> —MATTHEW 8:16–17

> These signs will accompany those who believe…they will place their hands on sick people, and they will get well.
>
> —MARK 16:17–18

> Is any one of you sick? He should call the elders of the church to pray over him and anoint him with oil in the name of the Lord. And the prayer offered in faith will make the sick person well.
>
> —JAMES 5:14–15

These last few verses as well as others we looked at earlier are important because they show that our healing is not just reserved for heaven but for here as well. While we may not know the Lord's method or timetable for healing someone, we can be sure that His Word tells us it is His will to heal us.

As I travel and pray over people for healing, I have noticed something very profound. It seems that very often the Lord will heal unbelievers and even new Christians who don't have any belief in healing just to show them He is real and loves them, but He holds those who have been Christians for a time to a higher standard. It is as though He is holding them accountable to knowing and believing what the Bible says about this subject, and He expects them to have faith in order to get healed. It doesn't always happen this way, but it is a pattern I have noticed at times. This could also be why Jesus only mentioned to some of the people He healed that their faith had made them well and not to all of the people.

It's All About His Love

One night while I was ministering in a big city, something happened that really shows what God healing our physical giants is all about. After preaching, I gave a short salvation message and asked who wanted to stand to receive Jesus. Only one person in the place stood. It was a woman who was sitting almost all the way in the back. She had come in late, and by the way she looked, it was obvious she had lived a hard life and still was.

After the salvation segment I ended the general service by doing a mass prayer for all types of healing over the whole place. We have seen the Lord really do some astounding miracles during that time, so I will often keep my eyes open during that prayer just in case I might get to see something happen. I noticed as I prayed, the woman who had received Jesus turned around in her chair a few times and even stood up and then sat back down once.

I ended my mass prayer and opened up the altar for those who would like individual prayer, and people flooded to the front. After about two hours that same woman had made her way through the line and was now standing in front of me. I congratulated her for asking Jesus into her heart and told her it was the most important decision she would ever make in her life. I asked her what her prayer request was, and she told me she didn't need any prayer, but she had a question for me.

She explained that when I started to pray for the group, she felt someone put his hand on her back, but when she turned around, no one was there. She said she had a bad back and it caused her a lot of pain. All of a sudden that hand went to the exact spot her back hurt the worst and began to gently caress and rub it. She turned around again but still couldn't see anyone, so it spooked her. She got up to leave but then realized the pain was now completely gone from her back, so she sat down again.

She said she also had a bad kidney, and it too caused her a lot of pain. After she sat back down, she felt that same hand touch her side. The pain instantly left her kidney as well. She then looked me in the eye very seriously and announced that she wasn't crazy and wanted to know what had happened to her. God immediately told me to tell her He was just showing her how much He loved her.

She got a very puzzled look on her face and said, "Why would He love someone like me?" I was then able to tell her it was because He had created her and she was His child, His daughter.

It is because of that love that healing miracles happen today. It is also because of that love we can trust Him to hear and answer our prayers as we come against the physical giants of this life.

Chapter 14

Emotional Problems

Minds Mended and Hearts Made Whole

A FEW YEARS AGO I received a phone call from a middle-aged woman who had inoperable breast cancer and had been given just a short time to live over two years earlier but was miraculously still holding on. She went on to say her cancer was so far progressed that one of her breasts was very disfigured and had actually ruptured, causing a foul discharge to leak out of it. The doctors told her they couldn't do anything for her except keep her comfortable with pain medicine, so she decided to just go back home and die there.

She had seen my testimony on TV and thought if God could save me, maybe He would help her, so she was calling for prayer. Even before I began to pray for her, the Lord kept telling me she didn't know how much He loved her. So once I started to pray, I told her what the Lord had said. Then He told me to tell her He was her "Daddy." Now let me stop right there and say that I know there are people who refer to God as their "Daddy," but I have never been one of those people. In fact, I have to admit that sometimes in the past it has even made me a little uncomfortable when someone around me has referred to God as their "Daddy," but I am starting to get over that now.

Because of my own hang-up with that term at the time I hesitated saying it, but the Lord told me again to tell her He was her "Daddy." I finally obeyed, and as soon as I did, He said, "Say it again." I did, and He said, "Say it again." So, over and over, I said, "God says He's your Daddy. God wants you to know He's your Daddy. God says He's your Daddy and He loves you." I'm not sure how many times the Lord had me say it when all of a sudden the woman broke down sobbing.

She said she was raised to believe in God and had since she was young, but she never had a father, so it was hard to understand a father's love for her. As a little girl she had prayed every day for a "daddy" but never got one, so it was also hard to believe God really loved her either.

We continued to pray when all of a sudden the Lord gave me the most amazing vision. I saw Him dancing with a little black girl who looked to be about eight to ten years old. She was in a pretty little red dress, and they were holding on to each other's hands and dancing in circles. As they did, the dress was gently swishing this way and that. He was looking at her with so much love and pride it was overwhelming to see, and I began to weep.

I started to pray in my head for her to be able to see the vision because it was so powerful. I knew if she could just see it, she would understand how much He loved her even as a child. Before I could stop myself, I started to pray aloud very passionately for her to see the vision. I finally asked her if she could see it, and she didn't say anything. I prayed some more for the Lord to show her, and then asked her again, "Do you see it? She's in a red dress." At once she said, "Oh, my God, I see it! It's on my wall." So I began to loudly thank God for the open vision I assumed the Lord was now giving her, and she said, "No, you don't understand. It's a painting on my wall above my bed."

She said that right after she had gotten cancer, a friend of hers was at a flea market and came across this one of a kind painting of Jesus dancing with a little black girl in a red dress. He was looking down at her with the most incredible amount of love, and the friend felt like she was supposed to buy the painting and give it to this woman to show her how much God loved her.

The Lord then told me to tell her when she was a little girl praying for a daddy, He was right there with her and had never left her. That's why He had sent this painting and vision. We both cried and laughed and praised God together on the phone for quite a while before hanging up. After I got off of the phone with her, I realized I never did pray about the cancer with her and for a moment was disappointed before the Lord spoke to me. He said that for her to know how much He loved her was the most important thing! That knowledge took away the lies that He didn't and it removed the pain in her heart. I had to think about that for several days before it really started to sink in. One thing it proved to me was that the Lord really wants to heal our emotional wounds.

Emotional Giants

The Bible tells us in 1 Thessalonians 5:23, "May God himself, the God of peace, sanctify you through and through. May your whole *spirit, soul and body* be kept blameless at the coming of our Lord Jesus Christ" (emphasis added). This verse shows us that we are a three-part being—spirit, soul, and body. This is interesting considering the Bible says we are made in the image of God and He is a three-part being as well—Father, Son, and Holy Spirit.

It is obvious what our body is. It is our literal flesh and bone, but there tends to be a little confusion when it comes to our spirit and soul. Some people even use those two words interchangeably, but it is clear from the Bible, as we just read in 2 Thessalonians, that they are two different things. As I researched this and read and reread each time these two words are used in the Bible, there appeared to be some areas of crossover leading to the confusion and different definitions given by Bible scholars.

Our spirit seems to define the eternal part of us that once we become saved is instantly reborn and belongs to God. Our soul appears to describe our will and emotions, which can affect our thoughts and attitudes, just as our spirit can. As we are a complex combination of these parts and might struggle to see the differentiation between them, it is interesting to see that the Word of God "penetrates even to dividing soul and spirit, joints and marrow; it judges the thoughts and attitudes of the heart" (Heb. 4:12).

The "soulish" area of us is where we encounter the emotional giants that can cause us so many problems. This can happen because, as we just read, our soul is able to influence our thoughts and attitudes and get into our heart and mind.

Some common emotional giants that people face are fear, anxiety, depression, sorrow, pride, anger, hate, jealousy, bitterness, greed, rebellion, guilt, shame, rejection, unworthiness, isolation, and doubt, just to name a few. As seen, these range from what a doctor might label a mental disorder to what a pastor might call a sinful pattern, so emotional giants cover a lot of area.

Once these emotions are embraced and fueled, they begin to affect our thoughts and attitudes on an ongoing basis until they become a stronghold in our life. At that point we are dealing with an emotional giant every bit as big as Goliath was.

In chapter 4 you read how I was dealing with the emotional giant of fear, and more specifically fear of man. I was afraid to go into ministry because of a fear of speaking in front of people, a fear of being called a hypocrite, and a fear of failing and looking foolish. You get the idea. I was consumed with fear, and it had become a stronghold in my life.

Demolishing Strongholds

The good news is that as we learned earlier, God gave us supernatural weapons to fight with, and they are able to demolish strongholds as well as any other giant that tries to rear its ugly head in your or my life. As 2 Corinthians 10:4 says, "The weapons we fight with are not weapons of the world. On the contrary, they have divine power to demolish strongholds."

So what does that look like? Well, when I stayed up that night engaged in prayer against the stronghold of fear, the Lord showed up and supernaturally removed it. He tells us in 2 Timothy 1:7, "For God has not given us a spirit of fear, but of power and love and of a sound mind" (NKJV).

Another great example would be from a nurse who called me one day for prayer. She had come to hear me speak at a church in her town and needed prayer, but because she had never seen people get prayed for like that at the kind of church she regularly attended, it made her uncomfortable and she didn't come forward.

She had battled with chronic depression for over eighteen years and was on the highest dosage of medicine possible, but she was still feeling miserable. She had very strong negative thoughts about herself and was always feeling guilt and shame even for things she had no control over. In fact, it was so bad she had gotten to the point of no longer wanting to go on and was calling as a last-ditch effort for help.

I explained that she had believed lies of the devil, and they had become a stronghold. I told her God thought she was valuable and He loved her. I then began to command the lies to be revealed and the stronghold of depression to be broken off of her in the name of Jesus.

I heard some strange noises over the phone and asked her what was going on. She said she could feel God working very powerfully and had begun to tremble and shake before falling on to her bed. She also said she had never experienced anything like that before, but she felt like a heavy weight had been taken off of her and she no longer felt depressed at the moment.

She called back over the following months to let me know she had come off all medication within one week, which she believed was a miracle in itself considering how high her dosage was and how long she had been taking it. She no longer felt depressed or had lasting negative thoughts about herself. More importantly, she had learned to recognize the lies of the enemy and reject them before they were able to become a stronghold in her life again.

In talking with her a few years later, I think the most touching part was now that this emotional giant had been defeated, she was able to finally feel the love of God in her heart and was getting closer to Him and learning to trust Him more all the time!

Exposing the Lies

The emotional giants people battle with can all end up getting traced back to some lie that the person has been tricked into believing. This applies to the obvious ones such as fear or depression, but it is just as true for the giants that could be labeled sin, such as jealousy or anger. The key then is in exposing the lie for what it is and replacing it with the truth. Our first example didn't believe God loved her because she never had a daddy, so that lie needed to be exposed and then replaced with the truth that He did. In the second example the enemy kept telling the woman what a bad person she was. That lie needed to be exposed so that she could see God had made her and valued her.

Very often the person who is struggling with the emotional giant has no idea how absurd the lie is they have believed because they have become deceived over time and can't see the truth.

Once I was ministering at a church, and as I prayed for the congregation, it seemed as though the Lord spoke to me about the pastor's wife. The problem was that what I was hearing went against logic to the point that I really doubted if I was hearing correctly.

To say that this woman was amazingly beautiful would have probably been an understatement. When she sang, she sounded like an angel. She also looked very confident and carried herself with dignity and class. But what I thought the Lord told me was that she had felt like "the ugly duckling" ever since she was a little girl and she felt too untalented and unworthy to do anything of value.

She didn't come forward for prayer, and because it seemed so crazy, I just discounted it. But at the final service her husband asked if I would pray for them together, and as I did, the Lord brought it to me again and told me to say it.

When I got close and whispered that she had felt unworthy and ugly since being a child and that God wanted to remove that lie right now, she literally collapsed to the floor sobbing. Later she explained that certain things had happened in childhood, and ever since that time she had believed those lies. Even the pastor looked surprised. Apparently this was a stronghold, or an emotional giant, she had kept well hidden for years.

Very often people become good at hiding these strongholds after enough people tell them how absurd it is, or in those cases when it is a sin issue they know it is wrong so they hide it from guilt or shame.

Taking Off the Masks

One night I had a dream that I was at a cookout in somebody's backyard. It was this small family and me. The dad was grilling, and as we talked, I had the sense that something was wrong with him. I couldn't put my finger on it as everything he said sounded fine. All of a sudden my viewpoint changed, and it was as if I were a fly sitting on the collar of his shirt. As I looked under his chin, I began to notice a faint line that ended up going around his whole face. I could now tell he was wearing a very elaborate mask, like the kind they would use in a Hollywood movie. I also noticed he was lightly sweating in his hairline, and then the dream ended.

I awoke, and the Holy Spirit told me that many Christians are wearing "masks" that are so good no one even realizes it. They say and do the right things, but it is not what is really in their heart as there are hidden strongholds of sin and other lies of the enemy they have bought into lurking there. Everything they say is filtered through the "mask," and even their own families don't know the truth. But the person knows deep inside, which is why the man in my dream was sweating. He was fearful of being found out he wasn't who he appeared to be and didn't believe everything he said he did.

That morning I spoke at a church and after preaching shared this dream. Then the Lord told me to say that if anyone wanted Him to remove their mask, they were to come to the altar and He would do that for them. No one was going to pray over them as this was going to be a sovereign act of God. It didn't matter if the mask was for always feeling like they had to say things that weren't in their heart, always feeling like they had to appear as something they weren't, for hiding lies they believed, or even for hiding flagrant sin. God was ready to take those masks off if they would let Him, and then He would demolish the strongholds that were there.

I was shocked as the altar began to fill up with individuals and the power of God hit the place. As the people came forward, several dropped to the ground and began to sob. Others were crying out to God for forgiveness, and still others hung their heads in somber silence. Some were standing, some were kneeling, and some had fallen prostrate. But their position wasn't the important thing. The important thing was they chose to come forward and let God remove the masks and demolish the strongholds—the emotional giants they were fighting against.

Know this: God wants to demolish the strongholds that have tried to entrench themselves in your life just as much as He did for those people that day. The great news is He is willing and able to do it right now if you ask Him to. It doesn't matter if your emotional giant is so big it can't be hidden or if it is tucked away under a mask. God wants to expose the lies of the enemy and instead plant His truth in your heart, soul, and mind so that you are set free!

Chapter 15

Financial Problems

No Recession in God's Economy!

A FTER THE VERY first time I was on a TV show that was aired internationally, I began to get phones calls from all over asking if Bruce Carlson (the man who prayed for me when the creative miracle happened) and I would be available to come and minister. One of those people was John Frederick, an Eastern Catholic Orthodox priest from just outside of Honolulu, Hawaii. He said he was trying to teach his church about God still doing miracles today and wanted us to be able to come in and share the testimony, proving the point. The church was kind of small, so his hopes were to be able to get some other area churches interested so they could share the expenses and planning in order to set up some meetings and get us out there. He was very excited and said he believed connecting with me was a "God thing" and an answer to his prayers.

Some weeks later he called me back sounding very disappointed. He said that none of the other local churches were interested enough in having us that they wanted to share in the expenses or planning, and his church was too small to be able to afford it. He concluded that he must not have heard God as he thought he did and apologized for wasting my time. I told him we should pray about it and see what God had planned, so we prayed on the phone and asked the Lord to send someone who would be able to arrange some meetings and get other churches involved—if that was His will.

Three days later my phone rang, and when I looked at the number before answering it, I saw it was from Honolulu, Hawaii, so I assumed it was the priest calling me back again. When I answered, I was surprised to hear a different voice. The man said his name was Aaron, and he had seen me on TV some time ago and then ordered my book *Saved by Angels* and was very blessed by it. That morning he was driving along, and the power and presence of God came into his car so strong he began to weep uncontrollably and had to pull over. The Lord then told him he was to call me, so he went home and looked in the back of the book and called our number out of obedience. He didn't know why he was calling and asked if I knew.

I was able to tell him I knew exactly why he was calling and then told him what we had prayed for three days earlier. After that we both cried because it was obvious the Lord was doing something grand. It turns out that Aaron was a successful business owner who was also involved in various ministries and had connections in different churches around that island. Not only did he set up and plan several meetings, but he also bought both Bruce Carlson's and my plane tickets and hosted us at his house.

I had always wanted to go to Hawaii but was disappointed that I wouldn't be able to share the experience with my family. A few days later some friends of ours stopped by the house and said that the Lord had told them to pay for a plane ticket so that one of our children could go along on the Hawaii trip with me. I thanked them for the offer but said it wouldn't be right to take it, and besides, it would be hard to just take one and not the other three as they were all so close in age. The couple seemed to get slightly offended and said that God had told them to do it and that was that.

I begrudgingly accepted the gift from them, and after they left, I told my wife I didn't know what we were going to do about it. A few days later someone else contacted us and said the Lord told them to pay for one ticket so that one of our children could go with me to Hawaii. By the end of the week four different families who had not ever once discussed it with each other had each given the money so that all four of our kids could go along. This only left the ticket for Lori, and a man from the other side of the country who didn't even know anything about the trip sent us some money and said we were to use it for whatever we wanted.

The meetings went well, and after five days of ministry we got to enjoy four days of vacation hosted and guided by Aaron and his wife, Min, who turned into great friends.

The priest was very happy with how things turned out and seemed to be happy most of all because of the supernatural way the Lord had answered his prayers through an obedient man named Aaron. I was also in awe of how the Lord had supernaturally supplied tickets for the rest of the family to go when I hadn't even prayed for it. I wrongly thought that it would be too selfish of a prayer. Lori told me later that as soon as she heard about the trip, she began praying for her and the children to be able to come along somehow and knew that the gifted tickets from our amazing friends were answers to her prayers!

Financial Giants

People need food to eat, clothes to wear, and a place to sleep. We also have wants that tug at our heart that can range from legitimate to excessive. Every person who has ever lived or will ever live is going to have to face financial giants in some form or another. If you want to know if financial giants are real, just ask the homeless person, a hungry person, or a person who has just lost their job or had their house foreclosed on.

Even people who are comfortable or wealthy still face financial giants as they are then tempted or forced to worry about keeping or maintaining their wealth. I have met many wealthy people who are more worried about money than most homeless people I have met. From third-world countries to Western nations, financial giants are alive and well.

It was obviously clear to God that money was going to be an area that would cause problems for us, because the Bible has a lot to say about issues related to money. One verse that is often quoted is from 1 Timothy 6:10. It says, "For the love of money is a root of all kinds of evil." Through the years some have misinterpreted this to say that money is evil or even that being prosperous is evil, but that is not what it says. It says the *love* of money is evil.

When Jesus gave His Sermon on the Mount, He also talked about money and making sure it didn't become too important to us. He made this statement in Matthew 6:21: "For where your treasure is, there your heart will be also." Then three verses later He says, "You cannot serve both God and Money." Jesus was clearly saying that any time money becomes too important to us, it turns into a financial giant because it takes our focus off of God.

That being said, it is still necessary to have money so that we can meet our daily needs. Jesus knew that too, and that is why He goes on to say that we don't need to worry about what we are going to eat, drink, or wear, because God knows our needs and will provide them. He then ends the subject with this beautiful promise in verse 33, "But seek first his kingdom and his righteousness, and all these things will be given to you as well." God knows the financial giants we will face in this life and is ready to take care of them for us as we put our focus on Him and do what He tells us to.

Focus on God

A dear friend of mine who has now gone to be with the Lord told me a great testimony that really proves what Jesus was saying.

This man had been raised in a Christian home, but once he moved out and got married, he quit going to church. He ended up getting divorced from his wife and really began to go through some rough times emotionally, spiritually, and financially. At one point he was living in a small trailer out in the woods and was driving a ways to get to a job that didn't cover his bills.

He woke up one Sunday morning hungry, but he didn't have any food and had just used his last few dollars to put gas in his truck and wouldn't get paid again until the following Friday. He decided to go down the road to a nearby lake just for something to do and began to throw stones in the water. He had been raised to believe in God and thought he did, but over the last few years he was having doubts. As he threw stones in the water, his belly was growling from hunger and he said, "God, if You are real, I would like something to eat. I think that strawberry shortcake sure would taste good right about now."

He began to think about what it was like going to church as a child and felt led to drive a few miles up the road to a little church he had seen in the next town. When he got there, the Sunday service was well under way, so he slipped into the last pew and caught the end of the sermon. He decided he would sneak out just before the service ended so he wouldn't have to talk with anybody, but as he was going out the door, an elder stopped him and introduced himself. My friend didn't want to be rude, so he talked with the man a bit, and by that time the other people were now filing out of the church.

The man said that he and his wife had invited a few people over to their house to have coffee after church and asked if my friend would be so kind as to join them. He ended up saying yes as he had nothing else to do anyway and went to their house with the other people. After they had talked awhile, the wife left the room and came back from the kitchen holding one plate of strawberry shortcake and put it down in front of my friend. She said they had it for dessert the night before and only had one portion left, but she kept feeling as though she was supposed to give it to him for some reason.

My friend said he ate it with tears in his eyes, knowing that God had answered his prayer and was showing him He was real and did care about his needs. He also realized God was showing him he needed to seek Him out first and foremost if he wanted peace in his life, and if he did, his needs would be met as well. During the following years he became a mighty man of God and ended up starting several jail ministries in the state of Wisconsin and touching thousands of people for the kingdom. These are the kinds of things that happen when God gets our priorities focused onto Him. When we do, He makes sure to meet our needs.

Let me share another testimony that fits right in with this.

One day a man called asking for prayer. He said he had been looking to buy a house on a certain block of a large city for ten years. In one week two houses went up for sale on that block, and he wasn't sure which one he should buy. After all that time waiting he didn't want to make the wrong decision, and this issue was really stressing him out. We began to pray, and the Holy Spirit immediately impressed upon my heart the real issue was that this man's relationship with the Lord was lacking. I stopped praying, and after asking some questions, it came out that he didn't regularly attend church and wasn't really active in his relationship with God. We talked about the importance of that, and afterward I began to pray again, and then the Lord told me he was to buy the house with the "blue trim." I asked him which house had blue trim on it somewhere and he said neither, but the Holy Spirit said he was wrong.

I told him to go look carefully at both houses again and then call me back. The next day he called back and said that one of the rooms in one of the houses had blue trim in it, but it had been repainted and the only way he even knew was because whoever repainted it had not repainted the trim inside of the closet where the trim was still plainly blue. He then went on to say that he just didn't know what to do. I reminded him we had prayed and God had clearly answered. So it was back to issue number one: his relationship with God. He couldn't trust because he wasn't close to God and didn't have the kind of relationship where he could hear Him when He spoke.

He ended up buying the house that had the "blue trim," and even though both houses were fairly close in price originally, he was able to purchase this one substantially cheaper after negotiating on it. The Lord answered his prayer for guidance and also blessed him, but not until He let him know He wanted more of a relationship with him. The Lord doesn't want us to have to stress out about financial giants. He wants us to focus on Him and know that we can trust Him.

Trusting Him

You read in chapter 5 how the first few years after my accident we used up all of our money and resources and were facing some huge financial giants. Then after the second year in ministry we started to get a salary, but it didn't even cover our bills, and gradually each year after that it increased until it finally was able to support us. That being said, the Lord made it clear in the very beginning of our ministry that when we ministered in a place, we were to never ask for any set amount of money. Instead we were to pray if we were to accept the invitation, and if we were, He would make sure to provide the money needed for the ministry and our family.

This means that the ministry has always been a 100 percent faith walk and still is, because we depend on the Lord to supernaturally meet all the needs of what He has called us to do—preaching, orphanage support, free book ministry to poor and jails, and so on—besides provide the salary to support our family. At times there are some large expenditures required in order to do what the Lord has called us to do, and I have to admit that occasionally I have let it stress me out a bit—nothing like I used to, but I have caught myself praying anxiously more than a few times.

One month the Lord told me we were to sow a significant amount of money into a few other ministries for things they were doing.

We obeyed, but not much money was coming in and I began to get concerned about it. I found myself lying prostrate on the floor for quite a while reminding the Lord of all the bills we had coming due when all of a sudden I unexpectedly went into a vision.

I saw a rough-looking field with rocks and tall grass. Then I saw a man from a long time ago with a brown leather bag over his shoulder walking in the field. He bent down and did something in the grass and then stood up and looked up to heaven with a questioning look on his face before moving on. The vision ended, and I asked the Lord what it was.

He told me to get up off of the floor and go stand outside in my driveway and look at the large oak trees in my yard. When we built our house on this piece of land, I purposely positioned it so that it would be right in the middle of these huge oak trees as I loved them so much and enjoyed the wildlife they attracted. As I looked at the trees, the Lord told me the vision was of the day He had one of His children plant those trees. I marveled at the thought knowing that the trees were over one hundred years old. Then the Lord told me something that absolutely blew my mind. He said He was thinking of me that day. He had that man plant those trees for me!

I burst into tears as I realized what He was telling me. If He had someone plant trees over one hundred years ago just for me because He knew I would enjoy them, then He knew what bills were due now and how He was going to take care of them. That kind of love meant I could trust Him. So can you because the Bible says that He loves all of us.

God Wants to Bless You

God made a statement through the apostle Paul to you and me in Philippians 4:19. It says, "And my God shall supply all your need according to His riches in glory by Christ Jesus" (NKJV). He says He is going to supply all of our needs according to His riches, and just for the record, He's not broke and there is no recession in His economy! For example, He tells us in Haggai 2:8 that He owns all the silver and gold. Somebody else might be holding on to it for Him, but make no mistake; He is in control of it. Just so there is no confusion about that, He says in Psalm 50:12, "The world is mine, and all that is in it."

God is not the author of lack. Our enemy the devil is. As Jesus said, the enemy comes only to *steal*, kill, and destroy, but He came that we might have life and have it to the full—the abundant life (John 10:10).

We read in Deuteronomy 8:18, "But remember the LORD your God, for it is he who gives you the ability to produce wealth, and so confirms his covenant." Later in Deuteronomy 28:1–14 we read how this was accomplished through several different blessings. This promise was originally just for the Israelites, but we know from reading the New Testament that those promises also apply to us now. Instead of getting them through following the Law as they did, we get them from having faith. (See Galatians 3.)

Just like with any other giants we might face in this life, we need to get God's promises planted down deep in our hearts so that we can know what His will is in the situation and fight from a place of faith and victory. We have to believe God wants to prosper us; otherwise we will be deceived into thinking He doesn't and won't stand in faith for what He has for us.

God desires to bless and prosper His children because He loves them, but there is also another reason we need to remember that is just as important. God expects His people to be a blessing to others, and we can't be a blessing if we aren't blessed ourselves, financially or otherwise. Third John 2 says, "Beloved, I pray that you may prosper in all things and be in health just as your soul prospers" (NKJV).

Conclusion

A s the Lord began to reveal truths to me from the account of David and Goliath found in 1 Samuel 17, I was astounded when I realized just how prophetic they were for believers today.

The first thing the Lord showed me from this narrative was that as we move forward in life, each one of us is going to face situations or giants of adversity that will seem too big to overcome. They will be towering and terrifying. They will shout at us and tell us they are even bigger than God or His power to help us. They will be loud. They won't stop yelling or go away, like the nagging depression, the constant pain, the broken marriage, the addiction, the overdrawn checking account, or anything else that you might be facing in your life. (See 1 Samuel 17:1–11.)

The following detail that became apparent is that God is looking for warriors. These are going to be people like Bruce Carlson who simply believe God's promises more than the threats of the enemy or any circumstances they might be facing. Seeing or experiencing the injustices of the enemy in their lives or the lives of others stirs up something inside of them that makes them want to do something about it. They are driven to then take action and not give up. God also made it clear that He doesn't force or "draft" His warriors. It is a freewill choice for each of us to be one or not. David made the decision to be a warrior, while the others did not. You too can choose this day to be a warrior, as this is God's will for all people. God said in Romans 8 that you are more than a conqueror! (See 1 Samuel 17:12–32.)

The next important point that came out was that as God's people lived life, they would go through trials or struggles that God could use to make them more mature and complete. This shows our spiritual maturity happens not in spite of our hardships but most often because of them. After going through a skirmish and seeing how God brought them through it, they would then have more faith and be able to believe that God would be there for them despite anything else the enemy served up.

One example from my life could be how after being molested I called out to Jesus and He hugged me and poured out His love on me. This experience then gave me the knowledge that I could always call out to Him and know He was there for me. David knew that because the Lord had delivered him from the lion and the bear in the past, He could be trusted to help him in this current situation with Goliath as well. What situations has the Lord brought you through that show you can trust Him? (See 1 Samuel 17:33–37.)

The next element that became clear was that the weapons God gives us for battle are not the same that the world uses. Second Corinthians 10:4 says this: "The weapons we fight with are not the weapons of the world." This means that sometimes people on our side as well as the other side might not understand or agree with what we are doing.

After I was physically well enough to work as a mechanic again, there were Christians and non-Christians alike who were offended that we chose to go into ministry and have faith in God to support us instead of going back to my old job. But we knew what He had told us to do. In much the same way both King Saul and even David's opponent Goliath thought David should have used "conventional" weapons. But David trusted God instead as he gathered the five stones from the brook. Have you received and embraced all five of the supernatural weapons that the Lord has made available to His children? (See 1 Samuel 17:38–48.)

Another important thing this encounter shows us is that we need to confront our giants head-on and not let them intimidate us so that we don't do anything, or worse, run away from them. For forty days in a row the two armies had faced each other. Each day the Israelites stepped up to the line desiring to overcome the giant, but his scare tactics prevailed, and each day they ended up backing down and running from him. When David showed up and faced the giant, the Bible says he ran to meet him. We need to do the same thing—confronting the giants we face in faith instead of fearing them or running from them! (See 1 Samuel 17:23–24, 49–51.)

One of the most exciting points we see from this account is that after fighting the giants and overcoming, there are rewards and promotion. Two different times it is recorded that David asks the question of what will be done for the man who slays this giant. (See verses 26, 30.) He later makes it clear that the reason he chose to fight the giant was not for the rewards but for the name of God. His priorities were in order (vv. 29, 45–47). That being said, after he killed the giant, he still received rewards and a great promotion. His whole life was changed after enduring the trial in the same way that Jesus's life was changed and he was instantly "promoted" into ministry after facing and defeating "giants" in the desert. (See Matthew 4.)

Realize that first David faced the lion and the bear before facing Goliath, before facing whole armies, and before becoming the king. Know that the giants and trials you are facing are preparing and training you for your future. Your victory over them will be the thing that transitions you to the next level!

Be Fully Equipped

David only used one of the stones to kill Goliath, but the Lord had him take five different ones along so he could be fully equipped. The fact that he placed the stones in an inner pouch of his shepherd's bag is prophetic of how the Lord wants us to receive all the weapons He has issued us and have them stored away in our heart so that we can always have them at hand. As David approached the battle line, he would be able to take out and use whatever specific one the Lord directed him to, like the smallest one for a long-distance shot or the biggest one for the closest shot. If he had only taken one large stone from the stream and the Lord then told him to take a long-distance shot, he would have been in big trouble as the stone wouldn't have made it there.

In the same way God has given the human body the five senses so it can be fully equipped for this life. If one or more of these senses are missing or not functional, it can be a huge disadvantage to the person. As we went through the five weapons the Lord has given us to demolish the giants in our lives, you might have realized you are accustomed to using some of them but not others. Maybe you know the Word but have a hard time praising God, or maybe you are used to praying but have never been taught to use the authority given us. If this is the case, you are at a disadvantage with your enemies. There will come a day when a giant is shouting at you and the Lord will tell you to pull out a specific weapon in order to defeat that giant, but if you aren't carrying it in your pouch, you won't be able to and will have to retreat.

Those five stones represented a complete arsenal of weapons the Lord wants to empower His children with. He knew we would need the whole assortment if we were to be victorious. Make an intentional decision this day to receive and embrace all the weapons the Lord has for us, and begin to make a habit of using them so you are fully prepared and comfortable with them. Each is designed to defeat the main tactics of the enemy, and if you find you struggle with one particular tactic the enemy uses, press into the specific weapon the Lord has given to defeat that tactic. The Lord has supplied everything we need to always be triumphant. This is no exaggeration, and His Word proves it in 2 Corinthians 2:14: "Now thanks be to God who *always* leads us in triumph in Christ" (NKJV, emphasis added).

Jesus said we will have tribulation in this world, so we know that the giants will come and just being a Christian isn't going to stop them from coming. The good news is He went on to say He had overcome the world for us, so we know that after the battle is over, we can enjoy victory and the lessons we were taught during the fight. Don't be confused; God is not the author of our trials, but He is big enough to be able to use them to our advantage.

If you embrace this message, it will change you forever as you go from glory to glory, living the miraculous life God has made available for all His children. The best part is we can then share this with a lost and hurting world, showing others how much God loves them and who He is as our lives overflow with His love and power.

Epilogue

How to Enter Into a Miraculous Life

O NE OF THE things we found was David had faith to fight Goliath that day because he understood he was in a covenant with the living God. He might have looked like a shepherd boy, but he knew he was a giant slayer, not because of anything he did but because of who his God was.

The five supernatural weapons we discussed and the testimonies you read about prove that Christians today can still have a covenant or agreement with the same living God David did. In fact, our covenant or "deal" is even better than his because we are under a covenant of grace and not law as he was, and the Holy Spirit is now available to everyone. (You can read more about this in Galatians 3 and the Book of Acts.)

The absolute best part about entering into this agreement is not the benefits we have while here on this earth, although they are great. The best part of this deal is when we make Jesus Christ the Lord and Savior of our life, we have the assurance that at the point of death when we pass from this life into the next, we will get to spend eternity with the God who loves us more than we can imagine.

In order for that to happen we need to know some things. One is that we are all sinners, and sin cannot enter heaven. Even if we are a "good" person, this is not enough (Rom. 3:20–23; 6:23). The good news is that Jesus died on the cross to pay the price for man's sin because of God's love for man (John 3:16; Rom. 3:24–25).

The next part almost sounds too good to be true, but the fact is, it is completely true. Romans 10:9 tells us, "That if you confess with your mouth, 'Jesus is Lord,' and believe in your heart that God raised him from the dead, you will be saved."

If you have never asked Jesus to forgive your sins and come into your heart, and you are willing to make Him the Lord of your life, then just say these words from a sincere heart right now:

> *Dear Jesus, I know I am a sinner. I have sinned against You and other people, and I am sorry for my sins and repent of them. I ask for and receive Your forgiveness today. Jesus, I invite You to be the Lord and Savior of my life, and I believe in my heart You died for the penalty of my sin on the cross and after three days were raised from the dead and are now seated in heaven. Lord, I ask You to send Your Holy Spirit to fill me to overflowing even now and that You melt me, mold me, and shape me into the person You want me to be. In Jesus's name I pray, amen.*

If you just prayed that prayer and meant it, then it is settled. You are now a child of God and are in covenant with Him. This is absolutely the most important decision you will ever make, and whether you felt anything or not, you are now "reborn" as Jesus said (John 3).

This is just the start of a new and exciting life. In order to help you along that journey, there are some things you should attempt to do almost immediately:

1. Find a church that teaches the Word of God and get involved.

2. Fellowship with mature believers who can help you to grow in your newfound faith.

3. Get water baptized and tell others what you have done.

4. Start reading the Bible daily and praying to God as you would talk to your best friend, knowing that He loves you.

5. Make the daily choice to live for God and honor Him through your obedience to Him and love for others.

Congratulations in your decision, and know that you have now entered into a miraculous life.

Appendix

Letter From God

ONE DAY WHILE attending a church service around the time I was finishing this book, a woman sitting directly behind me got this message or word from God that she delivered to the church. It so perfectly described much of the content of this book that I had it transcribed and have attached it here. I believe this was a message not just for the church that day, but for you, the readers of this book, and people everywhere.

My people,

Trials come; receive them as the opportunities they are: they are opportunities for you to try My faithfulness. Do not let life's hardships steal your joy. Know that I am able to work all things together for your good. I want you to remember, at all times and in all ways, I have your highest good in mind. I will never leave or abandon you. You must reject every thought that comes to make you think you are a spiritual orphan. I do not reject My children. Believe that I am breaking off every yoke of darkness that has been sent against your faith in My faithfulness to you.

The enemy comes to steal your strength and to sow seeds of abandonment during trials. But I am alive, I am active, I am powerful, and I am all knowing, kind, and faithful. That does not change when trials come. Reject all thoughts that are not in line with who I am. Faith is the ability to see with My heavenly eyes, believe with My heart, and believe that there is nothing I cannot do.

I want to transform your perceptions of what is going on around you. Have I not commanded you to take every thought captive? Hold each thought up to the light of My love, My faithfulness, and My promises.

In the coming days I will begin to take you to those places I describe in My Word as "glory to glory." Children, My desire is to make your life glorious. Come away with Me, into My presence, and listen to My heart. The more time you spend with Me, the more you know who I am and the more you will be able to discern what I am not. I desire to bring a newness, a childlike wonder to the things you discover in the secret place where I meet with you in prayer. Seek My face; believe that I desire to spend that time with you. Know there are many good things I desire to bring to your life, to bring through your hands to those around you.

I love you; I will never let you go. Did I not say you can "freely" receive all things I have given to you to receive? You have been made worthy to receive. So receive, even this day. Receive all that I have given. Come away with Me. Come away with Me.

My love has made your life glorious—My love and My provision. My life has been given so you could freely receive.

You are My dearly beloved child. I love you!

Sweet Bread Ministries

Sweet Bread Ministries is a nondenominational ministry dedicated to bringing people of all backgrounds into a closer, more intimate relationship with the Lord and the abundant life He offers us. We strive to do this through biblical preaching, teaching, prayer, and healing as well as orphanage support and free book ministry to jails and the poor. We are available to speak at your church, school, local correctional facility, or special event worldwide. We also offer one- and two-day seminars as well as prayer and revival services. Please contact us if you desire to see people get saved, healed, set free, and delivered by the power and love of Jesus.

Sweet Bread Ministries
230 State Highway 66
Rudolph, WI 54475

Phone: 715-213-6116
Website: sweetbreadministries.com
Email: questions@sweetbreadministries.com